Finding Your Way Around *Common Worship*

Finding Your Way Around
Common Worship:
A Simple Guide

Mark Earey

CHURCH HOUSE
PUBLISHING

Church House Publishing
Church House
Great Smith Street
London SW1P 3AZ

ISBN 978-0-7151-4236-3

Published 2011 by Church House Publishing
Copyright © Mark Earey 2011

Email: copyright@c-of-e.org.uk

The opinions expressed in this book are those of the author and do not
necessarily reflect the official policy of the General Synod or The
Archbishops' Council of the Church of England.

Typeset in 10pt Optima and Franklin Gothic by
RefineCatch Limited, Bungay, Suffolk
Printed in England by
CPI William Clowes, Beccles NR34 7TL

Contents

Contents

Abbreviations

ASB	*The Alternative Service Book 1980*
BCP	*Book of Common Prayer* (1662)
CHP	Church House Publishing
CI	*Common Worship: Christian Initiation*
CW	*Common Worship*
DP	*Common Worship: Daily Prayer*
FAQ	Frequently Asked Question
LEP	Local Ecumenical Partnership
NPW	*New Patterns for Worship*
OHP	overhead projector
PDF	Portable Document Format
PS	*Common Worship: Pastoral Services*
RCL	*Revised Common Lectionary*
RSCM	Royal School of Church Music
TS	*Common Worship: Times and Seasons*
VL	*Visual Liturgy*

Acknowledgements

This book has brought together material which I have been working on since the production of the first Praxis training packs in 1997. Consequently, I would like to acknowledge the support and encouragement of all those who have helped me to improve the teaching resources which I have been developing since then.

More recently, I would like to thank the students of the Queen's Foundation for Theological Education in Birmingham, who have been my frequent guinea pigs. In particular, I would like to thank the following: Sarah Bick, Wendy Biddington, Christine French, David Ford, Nancy Goodrich, Penny Harrison, Roberta Maxfield, Jo Morris, Judy Stote and Mandy Walker. Others who read early drafts of this document and were kind enough to make specific suggestions or to encourage me in the project include: Christopher Byworth, Anna DeLange, Alison Earey, James Hill, Peter Moger, Trevor Lloyd and Phillip Tovey. Members of the Group for Renewal of Worship were a great encouragement and urged me on when I was unsure about the value of the project. Finally I would like to thank Natalie Watson of Hymns Ancient and Modern, whose enthusiasm for the book has spurred me on to bring it to completion.

To all these I offer my sincere thanks: the book would have been much poorer without the help that they offered. What weaknesses remain are, of course, entirely of my making.

Mark Earey
Birmingham, autumn 2010

Foreword

Several years ago Mark Earey gave me a little insight into *Common Worship* which has stayed with me. He said that *Common Worship* is rather like a computer, with enormous capability, which many of us treat more like a word processor, with only very limited functions. That is certainly what I have observed around the Church. *Common Worship* is often used as little more than a facility for moving texts around an order of service. Certainly, that is part of what *Common Worship* provides – an opportunity for local and seasonal variety. But it has very much more to offer. It is not a larger and more flexible version of the *Book of Common Prayer*. It is a liturgical operating environment – a world of worship-making – into which we are invited to become accomplished technicians, confident linguists and skilled artists.

We will not travel very far into this liturgical world, with its multiple volumes and manifold options, without some help. The help we need is a kind of accompaniment – a source of wise and practical advice to which we can turn as we grow into the expansive possibilities of preparing and leading good worship. Now, thankfully, we have such a source within the covers of one short, practical and eminently readable book: *Finding Your Way Around* Common Worship*: A Simple Guide*.

Yes, it is a 'Simple Guide' and that is one of its great merits. True to any credible claim to simplicity, though, this practitioners' manual is a distillation of deep wisdom. It is rooted in a thorough understanding of the character, capability and complexity of *Common Worship* and it is written by (in my view) the best communicator of effective liturgical design and delivery in the Church of England. It helps that Mark is an engineer by training. He knows how one bit of something is connected to another, what it is doing and how the total system is meant to work. It also helps that he has had many years of writing and teaching about the different programs (to return to the computing analogy) of *Common Worship*; indeed he even had a significant hand in their creation. Most of all, it helps that Mark is a priest and pastor with a wealth of experience in preparing and leading worship in a whole variety of contexts from parishes, to theological colleges and courses, to large conferences.

This book is the product of those many skills and experiences. It is a real gift to us all and it is a gift worth grasping with both hands before you sit down to work the keyboard for your next bit of worship planning. It will answer all the questions about *Common Worship* that you were afraid to ask or did not even know you needed to ask. I hope that it will soon appear on the desk of everyone who is given the sacred responsibility of preparing forms of worship that will give glory to God, build up the people of God and make known the kingdom of God.

Christopher Cocksworth, Bishop of Coventry

Introduction

Common Worship has now been around for more than ten years. In that time it has become a familiar resource for worship in most, if not all, parishes in the Church of England, as well as in chapels in hospitals, prisons and schools. However, despite being much used, it is also peculiarly unknown. For many, it is encountered only through the *Common Worship* 'black book' and, for a significant number of congregations, it is not encountered even in that way, but only through a selection of locally produced service booklets or cards. This is not a bad thing: *Common Worship* was always intended to be used in this local and flexible way. However, if congregations might not necessarily be expected to be aware of the full scope of *Common Worship*, a more troubling reality is that many clergy and Readers (as well as other lay worship leaders) seem to have only a limited familiarity with the *Common Worship* range of resources – indeed, many seem unaware just how broad that range is.

I am regularly asked questions about *Common Worship* by experienced clergy and Readers, and by ordinands and others learning about Church of England worship. The questions are often surprisingly basic, and the answers are almost always there in *Common Worship* itself, if you know where to look. And that's the problem, of course. The first volumes of *Common Worship*, which came out around the year 2000, took up half a shelf, but some have been superseded, and all have been followed by more parts of the library, so that the 'full set' has been completed only in recent years. How is anyone expected to keep up with what there is, let alone know where to look in the library to find the answers? The result is that, unfortunately, '*Common Worship*' has become, for some in the Church of England, a byword for wordiness and complexity. The sheer amount of material is seen not as an abundant resource, but as a complicating constraint.

There's a danger, of course, that anything you write about it simply adds to that complexity, but the aim of this guide is to try to cut through the complexity with a focus on the basic things that users of *Common Worship* need to know in order to use it well. It is full of straightforward answers to common questions, all in one place. This is the 'manual' that should have come with the *Common Worship* library. It has been written with clergy and Readers in mind, especially those who are newly ordained or admitted. It might also help other leaders of worship in local churches. Its aim is to familiarize worship leaders with the basic information they need in order to make good decisions about how to use *Common Worship* in local settings.

This is not a history book or a commentary. The little bit of history that is included is only what is important in order to understand how to use *Common Worship* well. Similarly, it is not a practical book of creative ideas for how to use *Common Worship*. Instead, this is a more basic reference book – an introduction to the tools which *Common Worship* provides, for those who need to use them on a regular basis. Like all instruction manuals, its aim is to help users understand and use all the basic functions and to familiarize themselves with the more advanced options, ready for the time when they need them. For more thorough commentary and creative ideas you will need to look elsewhere, and I have suggested some ideas at the end of each chapter.

How to use this book

For some sections you might want to sit down with some of the *Common Worship* books in front of you as you read this book, but it has also been designed to make sense if you simply search for the particular issue that you want to check up on. For this reason, the Contents page and the Index are likely to be good starting places for most users most of the time. Because the book is designed to be dipped into in this way, some parts may seem a bit repetitive if you read it straight through. Whichever way you choose to use it, the aim is to get to the answers you need as straightforwardly as possible, so that you can get on with leading and planning worship which enables God's transforming love to take liturgical shape.

1

What is 'Common Worship'?

In most contexts *Common Worship* basically means the Church of England's modern services – that is, the services that sit alongside those in the *Book of Common Prayer* (1662) as the Church's basic liturgy. However, thinking of *Common Worship* as simply 'modern' services is not quite the whole story, because *Common Worship* also includes services which are in traditional language, and therefore don't necessarily *sound* modern.

A crucial thing to get straight is that *Common Worship* is *not* the name of a book. *Common Worship* certainly includes books, but it is a lot more than that. So if someone starts to talk about 'the Book of *Common Worship*' it's always worth making sure you know exactly what they are talking about (see below, p. 3: 'The *Common Worship* library'). The person in question might be referring to the 'black book' (sometimes known as the 'main' or 'core' volume), but they *might* mean the *Book of Common Prayer* of 1662 – that word '*Common*' in both titles has caused some confusion.

Where does *Common Worship* come from?

Common Worship is the current end-point of many decades of revision and experiment to produce services to be used alongside the *Book of Common Prayer* (*BCP*). To cut a long story very short, at the beginning of the twentieth century it became apparent that the *Book of Common Prayer* was no longer sufficient to cater for the breadth of worship required or desired within the Church of England. Because the Church of England is the established Church, any changes to the *BCP* had to be approved by Parliament. In 1928 and 1929 the Church produced a revised *Book of Common Prayer* (often called the 1928 Prayer Book), which Parliament rejected. This was the catalyst for a series of changes which resulted in 1966 in the Alternative Services Measure, which gave the Church the right to produce new services as long as they were *additional* alternatives to the *BCP*, rather than replacements for it. Thus Parliament retained control over the *BCP*, but the Church of England gained the ability to provide complementary worship resources appropriate for new contexts.

A series of services was then produced over the subsequent decades:

- Series 1 (1966).
- Series 2 (1967–68).
- Series 3 (1973–78) – the first in contemporary language (no more 'thees' and 'thous').
- *The Alternative Service Book 1980* (*ASB*) – which brought the alternative services to a temporary culmination in one definitive book.

Each set of services had a limited period of authorization, to make clear that they were experimental.

Common Worship replaced the *ASB* in 2000, when the *ASB*'s authorization ran out. Unlike previous alternative services, the *Common Worship* services are authorized 'until further resolution of the Synod', which means that there is no cut-off date by which they have to be revised again. If they are working, they can be left as they are; if they are not working, the parts that need revision can be looked at and changed or supplemented as necessary. In that sense, *Common Worship* is a work in progress, not a final answer.

Why is it called *Common Worship*?

The working title was 'Liturgy 2000', but it was important not to tie the services too tightly to a particular date, because, unlike the alternative services that had gone before, these did not have a fixed period of authorization – here, there was potential for something more long-lasting.

The title *Common Worship* was chosen as a deliberate echo of the *Book of Common Prayer*. In the midst of all the choices and flexibility built into *Common Worship* the Church wanted to signal that there was still an element of commonality, a 'family likeness'. This family likeness was seen as consisting of two elements:

- a clear structure;
- an 'evolving core' of common texts.

Who produces *Common Worship*?

Initial versions of any new services are produced by the Liturgical Commission, the Church of England's national liturgy committee. However, the Liturgical Commission produces material only at the request of the House of Bishops. Once drafts have been produced, this is just the starting point in a long process of experimental use in selected parishes and chaplaincies, and revision by the House of Bishops and the General Synod. The services can't be used generally until they have been authorized by the General Synod.

How to use *Common Worship*

The key to working with *Common Worship* is to recognize the importance of the shape or structure of the service. *Common Worship* starts from the premise that the shape of the service is more important than the particular texts in it. That's why every service begins with a page which sets out the structure. The idea is that by seeing the structure of the service the worship leaders will be better able to plan and lead the journey through the service.

The *Common Worship* library

Quick Tip: Getting *Common Worship* texts online

You should never need to type out any *Common Worship* texts. All the services are available for free from the Church of England website. You can access the texts there as standard web pages, complete with hyperlinks to take you to appropriate notes and other connections, but if you want them to be available on your own computer then it's best to download them in Portable Document Format (PDF – this is good for seeing it exactly as it is on the printed page).

From the Church of England homepage go to 'Prayer and Worship' > 'Worship' > 'Common Worship' and follow the links.

The 'main volume'

This volume is called *Common Worship: Services and Prayers for the Church of England.* Confusingly, this is also the generic title for the whole *Common Worship* library (it's built into the cross-shaped logo that is on the front of every volume of *Common Worship*).

People who have not been exposed to the full *Common Worship* library tend to think that there is just one 'Book of Common Worship', and it's usually the 'black book' that they are thinking of. One result of the confusion is that this volume tends to be known by several different names:

- The **standard volume** – this is slightly misleading because the same material is also available as a Desk Edition, and as Presentation editions (lots of ribbons and different coloured leather covers).
- The **Sunday volume** – because it contains the Communion services and non-eucharistic forms of worship for Sundays (that is, A Service of the Word, and Morning and Evening Prayer) as well as the basic Baptism Service and the Psalms.
- The **main volume** – because it contains the most frequently used services in churches on Sundays, and therefore is the basic book at the heart of the *Common Worship* library, and the one that was designed as the only book to be bought in bulk for the whole congregation in local churches and chaplaincies.
- The **core volume** – for similar reasons to above.
- The '**black book**' – because the basic hardback version of this volume is black. Unfortunately it's more complicated than that, because you can also get it in other colours (with leather covers) and because the Desk Edition (which contains the same material) is red.

In this book we'll call it the **main volume**.

Quick Tip: The Desk Edition

The Desk Edition of the main volume has the same contents and page numbering, but much larger print. If you want to lead services from the book, then it's worth investing in a copy, or having one to use at the lectern or holy table.

Here's a basic outline of contents of the main volume:

- The **Calendar** – a list of all the Sundays, festivals and special days in the Christian year.
- **Non-eucharistic Sunday worship** – that is, A Service of the Word, plus full versions of Morning and Evening Prayer for Sundays, Morning and Evening Prayer from the *BCP* (with the customary adaptations used in many parishes), and versions of Night Prayer (also known as Compline). This section also includes The Litany, Prayers for Various Occasions, some Confessions and some Creeds, and Affirmations of Faith.
- **Holy Communion** – Orders One and Two, plus some minimal supplementary material (if you want the full range of seasonal material, you need to look in *Common Worship: Times and Seasons* and *New Patterns for Worship*).
- **Thanksgiving** for the Gift of a Child.
- **Baptism** – the basic service, suitable for use as or with main Sunday services (you need to look at *Common Worship: Christian Initiation* for the full range of resources).
- **Collects** and **Post Communion Prayers** – the *Common Worship* set, in both contemporary and traditional language. It doesn't include the set of Additional Collects that was produced later – see below, p. 4.
- Rules for regulating Authorized Forms of Service – some general points (for example, hymns or silence can be used at other points than those indicated) and some rules for working out when festivals or special days come when it gets complicated.
- The **Lectionary** – for Sundays and principal festivals (*references only* – not Bible texts printed out). This gives the readings for the principal service and the second and third services.
- The **Psalter** – the *Common Worship* version of the Psalms.
- **Canticles**.

Quick Tip: Using the *Common Worship* main volume for Prayer Book services

The main volume deliberately includes Prayer Book material alongside modern services and texts. This can be useful in churches which use both sorts of service, and is also symbolic of an end to any perceived antagonism or even competition between modern and

---

traditional. The book reflects the reality of the Church of England – that both modern and traditional services continue to be used, often in the same local church or chapel context.

- Morning and Evening Prayer from *The Book of Common Prayer* (pp. 59ff.) – this is a good way of getting the feel for the shape and structure of the services, because they are laid out 'modern' style with clear headings and rubrics. It also includes the 'permitted variations', which means you can see how it is usually done in real churches.
- Prayers from the *Book of Common Prayer* (pp. 107–9) – includes prayers for the monarch and royal family and A General Thanksgiving.
- The Litany from the *Book of Common Prayer* (pp. 115ff.).
- Holy Communion Order Two (pp. 228ff.) – this is effectively 'Prayer Book Communion as actually done' so is a good way of getting the feel for the shape and structure of the service, and for seeing the bits that are often added (which are indented) or omitted.

The other volumes

The main volume is just the start. There's a whole lot more where that came from.

Common Worship: Pastoral Services

Dark green cover; large format hardback.

What do I need this for?

- Services and resources for Marriage, Funerals, Wholeness and Healing and Thanksgiving for the Gift of a Child.

Note that the current edition of the *Pastoral Services* volume is the second edition (2005). This edition includes at the end a section of Psalms for Use at Funeral and Memorial Services, and the Series One services of marriage and burial. These were not in the original 2000 edition, and so the page numbering of the two editions differs from p. 392 onwards.

Common Worship: Christian Initiation

Blue cover; large format hardback.

What do I need this for?

- Baptism, Confirmation, Affirmation of Baptismal Faith, and Reception into the Church of England.
- Also contains resources and services that can be used during preparation for initiation (Rites on the Way) and material for a corporate service of Penitence, individual Reconciliation of a Penitent, and a Celebration of Wholeness and Healing (for the full set of wholeness and healing resources you need the *Pastoral Services* volume).

Common Worship: Daily Prayer

Red cover; same size as the main volume. Available in hardback or with leather or imitation leather binding.

What do I need this for?

- Services of Morning, Evening and Night Prayer for use midweek (that is, not designed as main Sunday services).
- Also contains the shorter and simpler Prayer During the Day, plus the *Common Worship* Psalms and Canticles.

Common Worship: Times and Seasons

Orange cover; large format hardback.

What do I need this for?

- Seasonal resources. This includes some full services (for example, The Liturgy of Good Friday) and some resources that can be inserted into other services (for example, sets of intercessions for different seasons).

New Patterns for Worship

Maroon patterned cover; large format; hardback or paperback

What do I need this for?

- Thematic and Seasonal resources. Some of the material in *Times and Seasons* is also in *New Patterns for Worship*, but it is arranged differently. Seasonal material is included alongside other thematic material (for example, lament, creation). The book is arranged not by season but by function in the service (for example, greeting, confession, blessing).
- Training materials. Each section of *New Patterns for Worship* includes not only texts you can use but also training materials to help you produce your own material locally, and to train people to use it well.
- Sample services. A range of eucharistic and non-eucharistic services that are ready to be used and adapted, and to inspire your own ideas.

Though not technically named as a *Common Worship* volume, it is clearly part of the package, and the typeface and design marks it out as part of the same family of resources.

Common Worship: Festivals

Dark blue cover; large format hardback.

What do I need this for?

- Bringing together the 'propers' that the presiding minister might need for each of the Festivals (that is, basically the major saints' days) and Lesser Festivals. The propers typically include an Introduction to Confession, Kyrie forms of confession, Collect, Lectionary provision, Gospel Acclamations, forms of intercession, Introduction to the Peace, Prayer at the Preparation of the Table, Preface and Extended Preface for the Eucharistic Prayer, Post Communion Prayer, Blessing, Acclamation and Short Scripture Sentences. For some Festivals, and for the Lesser Festivals, the provision is limited to a Collect.
- Music for the Eucharistic Prayers – this repeats and supplements the material provided in the President's Edition (see below) for those who wish to sing all or parts of the Eucharistic Prayers.

This volume also includes the basic Order One Holy Communion service, with all eight Eucharistic Prayers, so that it can be used as the president's main book from which to lead a service of Holy Communion on one of these festivals. There is also similar provision for 'Special Occasions', which covers days and themes such as Rogation Days, Mission and Evangelism, Ministry, the Unity of the Church, Social Justice and Responsibility, etc.

Common Worship: Collects and Post Communions

Pale blue cover; large format slim hardback.

What do I need this for?

- Collects and Post Communions. This volume 'does what it says on the tin', and prints the original *Common Worship* Collects and Post Communions and the later set of Additional Collects on the same page to make it easier to make choices.

This book also includes the commentary on the Collects from the original 1997 volume, *The Christian Year: Calendar, Lectionary and Collects*, updated to include some explanation about the Additional Collects.

If you are looking for traditional language material, the Collects and Post Communions for Lesser Festivals, Common of the Saints and Special Occasions are published as a large format booklet.

Common Worship: Ordination Services

Maroon cover; large format; hardback or paperback; only published as a 'study edition'.

What do I need this for?

- Getting ordained, or planning and organizing an ordination service.

The study edition includes essays explaining the thinking behind the services and a practical guide to help those planning ordination services. It also includes the Ordinal from the *Book of Common Prayer*.

Common Worship: President's Edition

Red cover; huge format (pages are A4 size) hardback or leather bound and vastly expensive (don't forget you can download it for free). Designed for use at the holy table.

What do I need this for?

- Really large print versions of some material from the main volume – that is Holy Baptism, Collects and Post Communions, Holy Communion Orders One and Two, Supplementary texts (from both Holy Communion and A Service of the Word), Seasonal Provisions.
- *Additional* seasonal provisions, which are not in the main volume (that is, some short Proper Prefaces for Communion, and Blessings).
- Collects and Post Communions for Lesser Festivals (also now available in *Common Worship: Festivals* and in the booklet *Common Worship: Collects and Post Communions in Traditional Language*).
- Really large print versions of some of the 'propers' for Communion from the Pastoral Services volume (for example, introductions to confession, words at the peace, proper prefaces, blessings, etc. for Wholeness and Healing, Funeral, and Marriage services.
- Music for those who wish to sing all or part of the Eucharistic Prayers.

Where it reproduces items from the main volume, there is double-page numbering, so that you can refer congregation members to the page in the main volume if necessary.

Common Worship Times and Seasons: President's Edition for Holy Communion

Blue cover; huge format (pages are A4 size) hardback and vastly expensive (don't forget you can download it for free). Designed for use at the holy table, this is a revised and expanded edition of the original *President's Edition* (see above). The key difference is that this new edition includes material from *Common Worship: Times and Seasons* and it does not include traditional language texts.

What do I need this for?

- Really large-print versions of some material from the main volume and from *Common Worship: Times and Seasons* and *Common Worship: Festivals*.
- Collects and Post Communions, including the set of Additional Collects.
- Really large-print versions of some of the 'propers' for Communion from the *Pastoral Services* volume.
- Music for those who wish to sing all or part of the Eucharistic Prayers.

Note that although it includes material for Passiontide (including Palm Sunday) and the Easter season (including a fully worked-out service for a mid-morning Eucharist on Easter Sunday, based on the outline in *TS*) it does not include Holy Week and the Easter Liturgy, which are being published in a separate President's volume (see below).

Where it reproduces items from the main volume, there is double-page numbering, so that you can refer congregation members to the page in the main volume if necessary.

Common Worship: Holy Week and Easter

Dark red cover; large format hardback intended for the president to use (pages are squarer than A4 size to make it easier to keep open when used outdoors or in procession). It brings together material from *Common Worship: Times and Seasons* and standard texts needed for Holy Communion Order One.

What do I need this for?

- Large-print texts needed by the president at the services of Holy Week and at the Easter Liturgy (including a full order of service for a mid-morning Eucharist on Easter Sunday, based on the outline in *TS*).
- Music for the Easter Liturgy and for the Eucharistic Prayers.
- Large-print texts for The Way of the Cross and the Stations of the Resurrection.
- Large-print texts of the Passion Gospels (in both continuous and dramatic form, drawn from the *New Revised Standard Version* of the Bible in its anglicized edition).

Where it reproduces items from the main volume and from *Common Worship: Proclaiming the Passion*, there is double-page numbering.

Quick Tip: Finding what you need in the *Common Worship* volumes

Each volume has a main contents page at the beginning, of course, but there are other features that may help you find your way round:

- Each main section in the *Common Worship* books is marked by a solid red page, so as you flick through it's easy to spot the main sections.
- Many of the main sections have their own, more detailed, contents pages (that is, immediately after the solid red page) which may give you more of a clue.
- Don't forget that most of the volumes have a general index at the back and an index of biblical references.

And there's more

Don't forget all the other bits and pieces:

- Individual booklets for some services (for example, Marriage, Funeral, Holy Communion, Evening Prayer).
- Individual services on cards for the congregation (for example, Baptism, Thanksgiving for the Gift of a Child, Distribution of Communion at home or in hospital).
- Annual Lectionary booklets – give you the readings for each day of the current year, for Sundays and weekdays.
- *Common Worship* Weekday Lectionary (full, undated version) – only available for download from the web.
- *Public Worship with Communion by Extension* (London: Church House Publishing, 2001) – this material for extended communion is not officially a *Common Worship* volume, but follows the same style and uses *Common Worship* texts.
- *Common Worship: The Admission and Licensing of Readers* (London: Church House Publishing, 2007) – this material, 'commended' by the House of Bishops, is the first national (as opposed to diocesan) provision for the admission and licensing of Readers.

- *Common Worship: Proclaiming the Passion* (London: Church House Publishing, 2007) – a booklet containing the Passion Gospels set out for dramatic reading based on the *New Revised Standard Version* of the Bible. This seems to have not quite made it into *Common Worship: Times and Seasons*, but is helpfully available as a separate publication which can be bought for those taking part. The Passion accounts of Matthew, Mark and Luke are provided for Palm Sunday in the respective lectionary years, and John's Gospel for Good Friday.

And the ones that got away

There are a number of volumes in the *Common Worship* library that are now defunct. They are:

- *The Christian Year: Calendar, Lectionary and Collects* (London: Church House Publishing, 1997) – this blue-hardback book was the first of the so-called 'interim volumes' to appear, before it was even called *Common Worship*. It lives on in many a vestry, though its contents are now out of date in places (for instance, extra names have been added to the Calendar and some of the rules governing the dates of festivals and saints' days have been amended slightly). Everything in it can now be found in other volumes, except the Commentary on the Calendar and the Lectionary, which is only available via the Church of England website.
- *Common Worship: Initiation Services* (London: Church House Publishing, 1998) – this green paperback book was the preliminary edition of the initiation material. It has been superseded by *Common Worship: Christian Initiation*, which includes extra material and slightly more flexible rubrics about what can be omitted.
- *Common Worship: Daily Prayer – Preliminary Edition* (London: Church House Publishing, 2002) – this first, paperback edition was issued for experimental use to help the Liturgical Commission gather feedback which informed the production of the final edition (2005).

Common Worship and flexibility

Common Worship is designed to be used flexibly and creatively – that's why all of it is available in electronic form (via *Visual Liturgy* software and for free download from the Church of England website), so that you can adapt and use it in ways that make sense in your particular context.

FAQ – Can 'Fresh Expressions of Church' do what they like?

No, not if they are Fresh Expressions within the Church of England.

Some of the canonical requirements for what must happen in parish churches will not apply (for example, the requirement in Canon B 14 for Holy Communion to be celebrated each Sunday), but if the Fresh Expression is offering public worship then that worship should fulfil the requirements as much as any other Church of England service. What's more, any ordained clergy or licensed lay ministers involved will have promised to lead public worship using only forms which are authorized or allowed.

The Dioceses, Pastoral and Mission Measure of 2007 came with a Code of Practice to Part V: Mission Initiatives which specifically addresses worship in Fresh Expressions of Church (Appendix 3, The Ordering of Worship in Fresh Expressions of Church Under Bishops' Mission Orders). The Code basically works within the framework which applies to all Church of England worship. However, as the Code points out, there is much scope for flexibility within that framework, so read on for more detail.

Four types of material

One of the keys to understanding how *Common Worship* works is to understand the two basic categories and four basic types of worship material in the Church of England. Readers and ordained ministers have to promise that they will use only forms of service which are 'authorized or allowed by Canon'. Each of these categories ('authorized' and 'allowed') can be further divided:

Authorized		Allowed	
Prayer Book	**Authorized alternatives**	**Commended**	**Unofficial**
This means services in the *Book of Common Prayer* (1662)	This means a service which is *alternative* to something which is in the *Book of Common Prayer*. Some of *Common Worship* consists of alternatives to *BCP* services – for example, Funerals and Holy Communion services. These services have to be authorized by the General Synod of the Church of England. N.B. Diocesan bishops cannot give this permission on their own authority.	This means services or parts of services 'commended' by the House of Bishops as appropriate for situations where there is *no* authorized text (that is, nothing in the *BCP*, and therefore no need for an authorized alternative). Such services must be consistent with Church of England doctrine and be 'reverent and seemly' (Canon B 5). They are not compulsory (that is, other forms may be used). They may be brought to General Synod for debate, but they don't have to be authorized by the Synod. Some of *Common Worship* consists of services or elements of	This means anything else, such as songs, hymns, prayers and other liturgical material. It covers material which does not have to be authorized (because it is not an alternative to Prayer Book services), but which has not been particularly commended by the House of Bishops. The decision to use it is therefore a local decision, made by the minister or the local church council (or both). The official criteria are the same as for Commended services: they must be consistent with Church of England doctrine and 'reverent and seemly'. This would cover things like Iona or other liturgical

		services which are commended – for example, seasonal materials such as sets of intercessions, blessings, and introductions to the peace.	material, as long as it did not need to be authorized (so, intercessions would be acceptable, but Eucharistic Prayers would not).

Quick Tip: More flexibility than is obvious

Many of the *Common Worship* books contain a *mixture* of commended and authorized material. Each *Common Worship* book has a section which spells out which of the categories the different material fits into – see, for example, pp. 815–16 in the main volume. Just because it's in an official book, it doesn't necessarily mean it's the only thing you can use.

FAQ – Can I use material from other Anglican Provinces?

Possibly. You can use material which comes within the 'allowed' category. If it comes into the 'authorized' category, then you can use it only if it has also been authorized by the Church of England. Material which has been approved by other provinces in the Anglican Communion does not *automatically* count as authorized for the Church of England.

How do I know what I can use?

It can all get very complicated and painfully legalistic. In general terms, the key areas to take care over are these:

- Eucharistic Prayers.
- Confessions and Absolutions.
- Creeds and Affirmations of Faith.

These are particularly sensitive because they touch on areas about which there is doctrinal controversy (or, at least, disagreement) across the breadth of the Church of England. In particular, Eucharistic Prayers and Confessions touch on questions about ministry and ordination and the role of the priest.

Though these are the areas in which to be aware of the limits, it's also important to be aware of the freedoms and flexibility built into *Common Worship*.

Eucharistic Prayers

There are eight standard ones in *Common Worship Holy Communion Order One*, some with congregational responses, and lots of freedom over 'preface' material – see Section G in *New Patterns for Worship*. The Eucharistic Prayers for Use When Children are Present add more choices.

Confessions (and Absolutions)

See Section B in *NPW* for the complete authorized set of confessions and absolutions, including suggestions at the end of each confession about which absolutions would best complement it. The confessions include some which are responsorial, and there is also guidance about using flexible 'Kyrie Confessions', with 14 examples.

Creeds and Affirmations of Faith

See Section E in *NPW* for the full set of authorized ones, including responsive forms of 'standard' creeds, plus biblical Affirmations of Faith and a version of the Apostles' Creed suitable for singing as a hymn.

> **Quick Tip: Two key questions which determine the level of flexibility**
>
> There are two key questions to ask: is this for worship on a Sunday? If so, is this the Principal Service? The answers to these questions affect the level of local discretion. If the answer to both is 'Yes', then the options are more limited than if the answer to one or both is 'No'. See the table on pp. 49–50 for more information about what you have to include in a Service of the Word.

FAQ – Can I change the words?

With some parts of *Common Worship* (generally the commended material) you are free to adapt and change the words, as long as they remain consistent with Church of England doctrine and are 'reverent and seemly' (Canon B 5.3).

With authorized parts of *Common Worship*, the minister still has the right to make changes that are 'not of substantial importance' (Canon B 5.1), but there is little guidance about what a change of substantial importance means.

In practical terms (if you are using *Common Worship* books for the congregation), it is much easier to change words that the *minister* says rather than words the congregation says. If you are printing your own orders of service, or putting the words on a screen, then it is easier to make minor changes to the congregation's words too. However, once you've put changes on paper (or screen) you need to let worshippers know that what they are getting is not *Common Worship*. You also need to take care when changing well-known or much-loved forms of words.

FAQ – We're in a Local Ecumenical Partnership – does that make a difference?

Yes, it does. There are special rules for LEPs. You need to consult the ecumenical Canons (Canons B 43 and B 44) and the Ecumenical Relations Code of Practice. Your local ecumenical officer should be able to help you. In particular, the rules allow for a minister of another participating Church to baptize using the rites of that other Church, and for Church of England priests to preside at Holy Communion using the rite of another participating Church.

The printed book is not the full story

The way the services are printed out in the *Common Worship* books does not necessarily show you the only way they can be put together. You can often find your own answers to questions about what you can and can't do if you understand how to find your way round *Common Worship*.

For instance, a decision was made that in the main volume the path through Holy Communion would be kept simple, for the sake of those following the service in the book. Hence, though there are many possible positions for, say, confession, it is printed in only *one* place.

Before you assume that either the structure or the text is mandatory in the form in which it is printed, always make sure you have got a full feel for the service.

- Start with the **structure** page, which is normally at the beginning of the service.
- Then check the **Notes** which apply. These often contain extra permissions and are normally found at the *end* of the relevant section, but don't miss the General Notes on pp. 158–9 of the main volume.
- Finally, take a look at the **rubrics** (the instructions printed in red in the body of the service). Look for the word 'may' in the rubrics (for example, 'The president may use a seasonal blessing'; 'The Gloria in excelsis may be used') or for other flexibility (for example 'using these or other suitable words'). Rubrics also sometimes guide you to other pages for supplementary or alternative texts.

FAQ – Is it all right to use *Common Worship* material in my own printed order of service (or on our projection screen)?

Yes! The whole point of *Common Worship* is that it should be adapted to suit local contexts. There is no copyright problem about reproducing *Common Worship* material as long as the source is acknowledged appropriately.

Generally, an acknowledgement such as this will cover things nicely:

'*Common Worship*, material from which is included in this service, is copyright © The Archbishops' Council of the Church of England.'

For more information see *A Brief Guide to Liturgical Copyright* (3rd edition, 2000) (available to download from the Church of England website), and Mark Earey, *Producing Your Own Orders of Service* (London: Church House Publishing, 2000).

Further reading for this chapter

Paul Bradshaw (ed.), *A Companion to Common Worship – Vol. 1*, London: SPCK, 2001, Chapters 1 and 2.

Mark Earey and Gilly Myers (eds), *Common Worship Today – Study Edition*, Nottingham: St John's Extension Studies, 2007, Chapters 3, 6 and 7.

David Hebblethwaite, *Liturgical Revision in the Church of England 1984–2004*, Alcuin/GROW Joint Liturgical Study 57, Cambridge: Grove Books, 2004.

Peter Moger with Tim Lomax, *Crafting Common Worship: A Practical, Creative Guide to What's Possible*, London: Church House Publishing, 2009.

Michael Perham, *New Handbook of Pastoral Liturgy*, London: SPCK, 2000, Chapters 2, 3 and 4.

Michael Perham (ed.), *The Renewal of Common Prayer – GS Misc. 412*, London: Church House Publishing/SPCK, 1993, page 6 and Chapter 9 for more on the idea of an 'evolving core' of common texts.

Phillip Tovey, *Mapping Common Worship: Mind Maps to Find Your Way Round All the Volumes of Common Worship*, Grove Worship Series 195, Cambridge: Grove Books, 2008.

2

Calendar, Lectionary and Collects

The *Common Worship* Calendar

Quick Tip: 'Calendar' as a technical term

'Calendar' in this context means the seasons, Sundays and Festivals of the Christian year, as set out in *Common Worship*.

Services and resources to use alongside the Calendar

Common Worship: Times and Seasons is the obvious resource to use alongside the Calendar, as it provides resources and services for the key seasons of the year. However, don't forget that there is also useful seasonal material in *New Patterns for Worship*. The difference is in how the material is arranged. In *Times and Seasons* it is arranged by season, whereas in *New Patterns for Worship* it is arranged by position or function in the service (for example, all the confession material in one section) and is 'tagged' by theme rather than explicitly by season. There is a useful table on p. 59 (repeated on p. 501) of *New Patterns for Worship* which maps the thematic 'tags' onto matching seasons (for example, items marked with the theme of 'Cross' might be useful in Lent and Holy Week).

Liturgical colours and the Calendar

The use of liturgical colours (for instance, on vestments or frontals on the holy table) in the Church of England is not compulsory, but has the status simply of 'customary use' in many churches. Where colours are used, this is the typical pattern:

Colour	Seasons and Days
Green	Ordinary Time.
Purple	Advent, Lent (some churches use simple linen, also known as 'Lent array').
White or Gold	Christmas, Epiphany, Easter (that is, feasts of celebration). White can also be used for festivals, commemorations and saints who were not martyred.
Red	Pentecost, most of Holy Week and festivals of saints who were martyred (think 'fire' and 'blood'). Red can also be used in the pre-Advent period between All Saints (1 November) and Advent Sunday.

The liturgical colours are also sometimes used for particular events or types of service:

- Purple is often used for funerals (and some churches have black vestments for funerals too).
- White is usually used for weddings and is appropriate for baptism, confirmation and ordination services. There is also an argument for saying that it should be used for funerals (as the colour of resurrection) though this is more common at the funeral of a child than of an adult.
- Red is an alternative colour for services in which there is particular prayer for the Holy Spirit, such as baptism, confirmation or ordination services.
- Pink (technically 'rose-colour') is used in some churches on festivals which are or were traditionally related to the Blessed Virgin Mary (such as the Fourth Sunday of Lent and the Third Sunday of Advent).

For more detail on all of this, see the main volume, pp. 532–3, or *TS*, pp. 28–9.

FAQ – How do I know which colour to use?

The first step is to check on what local practice is, as there are no hard-and-fast rules about the use of colour in the Church of England.
   However, if you want some guidance there are two places to look:

- Appropriate colours are suggested next to the collects in the *Common Worship* books, so if you can find the right collect you should be able to find an appropriate colour.
- Colours are also suggested for each day of the year in the annual lectionary booklets (see below in the section about the Weekday Lectionary, p. 37).

The *Common Worship* way of structuring the year

Figure 1 gives a summary of the Christian year, as structured by the *Common Worship* Calendar. It has much in common with the Calendar in other Churches, but with some unique Church of England twists.
   To follow the diagram, start with Advent at the 12 o'clock position, and work round. For more detail, see the next section.

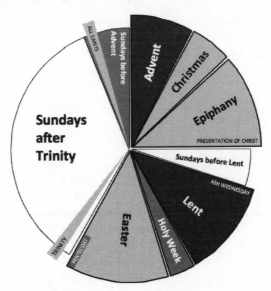

Figure 1: The Christian Year in Common Worship

Some key points about the Calendar

- The 'year' begins on the First Sunday of Advent (as it does in the *BCP* Calendar). This means that the different years of the Lectionary also start on that Sunday and not on 1 January.
- Sundays in a season are named Sundays *of* the season (for example, the Second Sunday of Christmas, the Third Sunday of Easter) rather than Sundays *after* a particular day.
- There are two periods of 'Ordinary Time' – one before Lent (that is, usually late February, March and early April), and another after Pentecost (that is, usually from late May or early June through to the end of November). These times are 'ordinary' in the sense that there is no seasonal emphasis.
- The Presentation of Christ in the Temple (sometimes called Candlemas or The Purification of the Blessed Virgin Mary) on 2 February (or the nearest Sunday to it) marks the concluding point of the Epiphany Season.
- If Easter is early, Sundays are 'lost' from the period of Ordinary Time before Lent, *not* from the Epiphany Sundays.

Quick Tip: Stations of the Cross

You'll find the Stations of the Cross in a section headed Way of the Cross in the Lent part of *Common Worship: Times and Seasons* (starting on p. 236). The form provided is a modern 15-station pattern, based entirely on the biblical accounts and concluding with the resurrection. The traditional 14 stations are listed on p. 256.

As a complement to the Way of the Cross, don't miss the new Stations of the Resurrection (*TS*, pp. 443–68) as a resource to use in the Easter season.

Quick Tip: Passion Gospels in Holy Week

Don't forget that you can get the Passion Gospels set out for dramatic reading on Palm Sunday and/or Good Friday in a booklet called *Common Worship: Proclaiming the Passion* (London: Church House Publishing, 2007). They are also reproduced (in both dramatic and continuous forms) in *Common Worship: Holy Week and Easter.*

- Pentecost is seen not as the start of a 'Spirit' season but as the Feast of the Holy Spirit, which concludes the season of Eastertide.
- The period from Ascension to Pentecost is seen as a mini-season of preparation for the celebration of the Spirit.
- Trinity Sunday is a Principal Feast, but does *not* mark the start of a season. Sundays in the second period of Ordinary Time are therefore Sundays *after* Trinity, rather than Sundays *of* Trinity, as there is no 'Trinity season'.
- If the date of a church building's dedication is not known, it may be celebrated on the first Sunday in October, or the Last Sunday after Trinity (but note: Bible Sunday may also be celebrated on the Last Sunday after Trinity – see box below).

Quick Tip: Bible Sunday has moved

Generations of Anglicans were used to the Second Sunday of Advent being 'Bible Sunday'. The Prayer Book Collect ('Blessed Lord, who hast caused all holy scriptures to be written for our learning; Grant that we may in such wise hear them, read, mark, learn and inwardly digest them . . . ') combined with the Epistle reading (Romans 15.4–13 – 'For whatever was written in former days was written for our instruction . . . ') made it a perfect match.

The *Common Worship* Calendar moves the collect about scripture to the Last Sunday after Trinity, making that date the most obvious one for an optional Bible Sunday. A set of readings is provided for churches which keep this as Bible Sunday (see *Common Worship* main volume, p. 575). This allows the Second Sunday of Advent to take on a more explicitly 'Advent' focus.

- The Sunday after All Saints may be called All Saints' Sunday (to encourage the theme of the saints to be taken up).
- The Sunday before Advent is called Christ the King.

Quick Tip: Red before Advent

The period from All Saints' Day (1 November) to the eve of Advent is technically part of the second period of Ordinary Time, but it has a special focus on the reign of Christ in earth and heaven. The liturgical colour can be red (rather than green) to reflect this.

N.B. Users of the earlier seasonal resource book, *The Promise of His Glory*, will recall that this time was called the Kingdom season. The same focus remains, but the title was seen as too restricting and is not used in *Common Worship*.

FAQ – Why does John the Baptist feature in the readings on both Advent 2 and Advent 3?

John the Baptist has a double significance at this time of year:

- his preaching of repentance prefigures the self-examination necessary in the light of the return of Christ to judge the living and the dead;
- the events surrounding his own birth are intimately associated with the events of the birth of Christ himself.

Levels of celebration

Certain days in the Calendar are given special emphasis as days of particular celebration or significance. There is a sliding scale of technical terms which show the respective levels of importance:

Level of significance	Examples	Implications for worship
Principal Feast or **Principal Holy Day**	Christmas Day, Easter Day, Ascension Day, All Saints' Day, Ash Wednesday, Maundy Thursday, Good Friday	Holy Communion is meant to be celebrated in all parish churches on these days (with the exception of Good Friday).

Festivals	The Conversion of Paul (25 January) Mary Magdalene (22 July) Christ the King (Sunday before Advent)	Most of these relate to particular dates. If the date clashes with a Principal Feast or Principal Holy Day, the Festival must be transferred to the next available day. If a Festival falls on any other Sunday, it can be kept on the Sunday or transferred to the next Monday. Readings and Collects are provided for these days.
Lesser Festivals	William Tyndale (6 October) Francis of Assisi (4 October) Hilda of Whitby (19 November) John Bunyan (30 August) Beheading of John the Baptist (29 August)	Each local church determines how much to make of these days. Individual collects are provided (in *DP* and the *President's Edition*). Readings are provided via the Common of the Saints (see below) for Holy Communion services, but not for Morning and Evening Prayer. If a Lesser Festival clashes with a Festival or Principal Feast or Holy Day it is normally omitted for that year.

Commemorations	George Fox (13 January) Oscar Romero (24 March) Christina Rossetti (27 April) Florence Nightingale (13 August) Cecilia (22 November)	These are optional and are remembered chiefly in the prayers or perhaps by a mention in the introduction to the service. They do not have individual sets of readings or Collects, but if these are required the Common of the Saints can be used.
Local Celebrations	Patron Saint of a church; Dedication Festival of a church (that is, the anniversary of the date of its dedication or consecration); Harvest Festival; particular diocesan commemorations	The dedication or the Patronal Festival can be kept either as a Festival or a Principal Feast.

For more detail on all of this, see the Rules to Order the Christian Year (main volume pp. 526–32; *TS*, pp. 24–8) and the associated table which gives detailed guidance about transferences when there is a clash of celebrations. To get a feel for how this works out across the year, see the lists of the Seasons and Holy Days (main volume, pp. 2–16; *TS*, pp. 8–22).

'Common of the Saints'

This is the title given to Collects, Bible readings and other propers (that is, specially appropriate texts) for whole categories of persons, rather than individuals (for example, Apostles and Evangelists; Martyrs; Members of Religious Communities). Similar resources are provided for Special

Occasions, which include more general themes such as Mission and Evangelism, The Unity of the Church, Social Justice and Responsibility, Harvest Thanksgiving and Rogation Days.

Where can I find the Common of the Saints?

Material for the Common of the Saints can be found in the following places:

- *Common Worship: Daily Prayer* – Suggested collects, canticles and refrains are given for the Saints on pp. 527–34 and for Special Occasions on pp. 535–45; material for Night Prayer is on pp. 356f.
- *Common Worship: President's Edition* – Collects and Post Communions are provided for Saints and for Special Occasions (contemporary language pp. 203–23; traditional language pp. 357–77). A small selection of other propers can be found on pp. 604–8.
- *Common Worship: Collects and Post Communions* – Collects and Post Communions in contemporary language are provided for Saints (pp. 155–64) and for Special Occasions (pp. 165–75).
- *Common Worship: Festivals* – Saints, pp. 267–329, and Special Occasions, pp. 331–67. This volume gives very comprehensive material in contemporary language for each category, such as forms of intercession, blessings, eucharistic material, Kyrie confessions, etc.

Common sets of Bible readings were originally published in the volume *The Christian Year: Calendar, Lectionary and Collects* (London: Church House Publishing, 1997), and have since been reproduced in the back of the annual Lectionary booklets. They give a selection of suitable readings for each category, plus one or two readings particularly appropriate for each Lesser Festival. These sets of readings can also be found in the Festivals volume, integrated into the collects and other liturgical texts for each category of saint or Special Occasion.

FAQ – How can I find the date of Easter?

There is a table which gives the dates of Ash Wednesday, Easter Day, Ascension Day, Pentecost and the First Sunday of Advent. The table is printed in the main volume on p. 17 (with dates going up to 2030) and in *TS* on p. 23 (with dates going up to 2040).

To find out which year of the lectionary you need (A, B, or C), see the table on p. 538 of the main volume.

The *Common Worship* Principal Service Lectionary

What is a lectionary?

A lectionary is simply a list of Bible readings assigned to each Sunday of the Christian year (and also to Festivals, saints' days and other special commemorations). It's a way of ensuring a reasonable coverage of the breadth of scripture over a period of time.

Where does it come from?

The *Common Worship* Lectionary is a slightly altered version of the *Revised Common Lectionary* (*RCL*). This is an internationally used ecumenical lectionary. The key dates are:

- 1969 – As a result of Vatican 2, the Roman Catholic Church produced a new lectionary that worked on a three-year pattern, and included more of the Bible.
- 1983 – The Consultation on Common Texts (a forum for worship renewal among churches in Canada and the USA) published an ecumenical version, the *Common Lectionary*.
- 1992 – A revised version, the *RCL*, was produced.
- 1997 – The Church of England published the *Common Worship* lectionary, based on the *RCL*.

What we are talking about here is technically the Principal Service Lectionary. This is the lectionary for the main service at a church on a Sunday. There are accompanying Lectionaries for a second and third service on a Sunday, called (imaginatively) the Second Service Lectionary and the Third Service Lectionary.

FAQ – Which service is the principal service?

There is no general rule about this. Each local church needs to decide which of its services on a Sunday will be treated as the principal service. *Common Worship* says that this decision is for 'the minister' to make (main volume, p. 540, Rule 8).

In many instances the principal service will simply be the main mid-morning service, which the largest number of persons attend, with the Second Service Lectionary being used for an evening service.

However, in many situations (for instance, a multi-parish benefice) the evening service might be the principal (or only) service. In other contexts, the numbers may be larger in the evening, but the morning still feels like the principal service.

Quick Tip: *Common Worship* compared with the *Revised Common Lectionary*

The *Common Worship* Principal Service Lectionary is almost the same as the *RCL*, but there are one or two Sundays where the readings differ. This makes a difference if you are using ecumenical material to help you with sermon preparation or choosing hymns or providing material for children's and youth groups. Make sure you check that the readings are the same before you use ecumenical material, and look out for any Sundays where there is special provision for the *Common Worship* version of the lectionary.

How does the Lectionary work?

The Principal Service Lectionary has a three-year cycle. Each year majors on one Synoptic Gospel:

- Matthew – Year A.
- Mark – Year B.
- Luke – Year C.

Each Lectionary 'year' starts on Advent Sunday, not 1 January.

FAQ – How do I know which Lectionary Year we're in?

The *Common Worship* main volume has a table giving the lectionary years (p. 538).

Advent Sunday 2011 marks the beginning of Year B; Advent Sunday 2012 begins Year C; Advent Sunday 2013 begins Year A; and so on.

Quick Tip: Lectionary readings printed out

You can buy copies of the lectionary (*RCL* and/or the *Common Worship* version) with the readings printed out in full in a particular Bible version. For instance:

- *The Common Worship Lectionary: New Revised Standard Version (Anglicized Edition)* (Oxford: Oxford University Press, 1999) – all three years, Principal Service only.
- *The Word of the Lord: Year A* (Norwich: Canterbury Press, 1999) – *Common Worship* readings for the Principal, Second and Third Services using the NRSV; in three volumes for years A, B and C, plus a volume for special occasions; large format, designed for use at the lectern as well as the desk.
- *Revised Common Lectionary in* NRSV *(Sundays and Festivals)* (London: Mowbray, 1997) – single volume, huge format for use in church; *RCL*, with *Common Worship* variations included.

The Lectionary connects with the Calendar because the Lectionary works differently in the seasons from the way it works in Ordinary Time.

The Lectionary readings

The Old Testament reading

Seasonal Time	Ordinary Time
Old Testament readings relate to the Gospel (preparing for it or prefiguring it). In the Easter Season, the book of Acts (rather than an OT book) is used as the first reading, followed by an epistle reading.	There is a twin-track approach: • A 'Continuous' track takes you through an OT book semi-continuously. • A 'Related' track provides OT passages which connect to the Gospel (as in Seasonal Time).

The Psalms

The Psalms are generally chosen to connect with the OT reading. Therefore, during Ordinary Time where there are two OT tracks, there are also two possible Psalms.

The New Testament reading

Seasonal Time	Ordinary Time
New Testament passages are usually semi-continuous, but may be chosen from a book which reflects the feel of the season. (For example, on the Sundays of Easter there are a series of readings from 1 Peter in Year A, 1 John in Year B and Revelation in Year C.)	New Testament passages are independent of the Gospel reading, and usually semi-continuous.

The Gospel reading

Seasonal Time	Ordinary Time
An appropriate passage from the Gospel of the year is used.	The Gospel of the year is read semi-continuously (that is, working through more or less chapter by chapter, omitting parts used in Seasonal Time).

This pattern is not followed rigidly – for instance, it would be hard to find appropriate Christmas readings in Year B from Mark's Gospel, which has no account of Jesus' birth.

John's Gospel is used in all three years, particularly before and after Easter (and more so in Year B, as Mark is a shorter Gospel than the others).

Quick Tip: What – no themes?

A key to understanding the *Common Worship* Lectionary is recognizing that the readings on any one Sunday are not necessarily connected closely to one another. So if you are struggling to spot the theme, it's probably because there isn't one. The secret with preaching from the Lectionary, therefore, is to pick one of the readings and major on that, rather than to try to tie the readings together neatly.

This can also make it harder to choose hymns and songs in advance – they may need to take account of which reading will be focused on in the sermon, rather than being chosen on the basis of a general 'theme' for the Sunday.

FAQ – Do we have to use the Lectionary?

Common Worship adopts the principle of 'open' and 'closed' Lectionary seasons. This allows for local choice of Bible readings during Ordinary Time, while preserving a sense of commonality across the Church of England (and ecumenically, with other churches which use the *RCL*) at the key seasons of the year.

The clearest advice on the 'open' and 'closed' seasons is given in *New Patterns for Worship*, Section C, pp. 103–4.

New Patterns for Worship Section C also includes a selection of 'Lectionary modules' which show the sort of thing that is possible in the open season. These are groups of readings spanning several weeks, focusing on a theme (for example, Meals in the Ministry of Jesus) or particular books or parts of the Bible (for example, the story of Joseph in Genesis, or the book of Habakkuk). They would make a good basis for a sermon series. The ones provided are just examples – you can also construct modules locally.

Understanding 'propers'

In the context of the lectionary, a 'proper' is a set of readings for a Sunday which falls between certain dates (for example, Proper 3 is the set of readings for the Sunday between 17 and 23 February – see the main volume, p. 549). Propers apply in Ordinary Time, when the Lectionary readings are determined by date, rather than by the liturgical name of the Sunday.

See below, 'How the Collects relate to the readings', p. 44, for more on this. Also note that 'proper' can mean something else in other contexts – see the entry in the Glossary for details.

FAQ – Do you have to use a particular version of the Bible for readings?

Readings in *Common Worship* services can be from any Bible version which is not prohibited (see the main volume, p. 539, Rule 1). Currently, no versions of the Bible are prohibited!

Quick Tip: Getting the verse numbers right

Although any Bible version can be used for readings, the Lectionary uses the verse numbering in the *New Revised Standard Version*, apart from the psalms, which follow the *Common Worship* Psalter.

The latter point is particularly useful to know if you use the *Common Worship* Lectionary, but read or sing the actual psalms from the *Book of Common Prayer*. If the Lectionary specifies that the psalm should start or finish at a particular verse, it will mean the *Common Worship* verse number, which is often different from the Prayer Book number.

FAQ – How many Bible readings must we have?

A Service of the Word requires two or, at the very least, one reading (main volume, p. 27, Note 5). For a non-eucharistic service there is no rule about which of the readings should be chosen.

If the service is a Sunday service and includes Holy Communion, then *Common Worship* encourages that 'whenever possible' three readings (Old Testament, New Testament and Gospel) are used, but recognizes that two may suffice (see the rubrics in the Holy Communion services and also Note 12 on p. 332 of the main volume). Of the two, one must be the Gospel reading (main volume, p. 540, Rules 6 and 8).

The Second and Third Service Lectionaries

The best way to understand the Second and Third Service Lectionaries is to realize that they don't mean the second or third service to take place in the course of a day, but second or third in 'significance'. The most significant service (the Principal Service) could be the third one in the day, on a Sunday evening.

The Second Service Lectionary is designed, typically, with an evening service in mind, where the Principal Service has been a Sunday morning service. The Third Service Lectionary assumes a small-scale daily office context, perhaps a Morning Prayer before a later Eucharist. However, in some contexts the pattern may be completely different, with the Principal Service happening in the evening and the Second Service Lectionary being used for a service of Morning Prayer or a small Holy Communion service. The Second Service Lectionary is always provided with a Gospel reading to allow for its use at the Eucharist.

Like the Principal Service Lectionary, the Second and Third Service Lectionaries work on a three-year cycle, though they do not follow the pattern of preferring a particular Gospel in each of the three years. However, in Ordinary Time the Third Service Lectionary has the same readings for each of the three years (though with different psalms).

The Weekday Lectionary

The *Common Worship* Weekday Lectionary gives three basic sets of readings:

- A daily Lectionary for Communion services – this works on a two-year cycle, and is based on the Roman Catholic Daily Eucharistic Lectionary.

- A daily Lectionary for Morning Prayer.
- A daily Lectionary for Evening Prayer.

The Morning and Evening Prayer Lectionary works on a two-year cycle, and the readings generally follow through sequentially from day to day (that is, the Morning Prayer New Testament readings might be working through Ephesians and the Evening Prayer readings working through Mark's Gospel). The readings swap annually, so that this year's readings at Morning Prayer will be next year's readings at Evening Prayer. In this way, the whole sequence is covered in one year if you use both Morning and Evening Prayer, and in two years if you use only one service a day.

Quick Tip: Bible reading notes for the Lectionary

You can get daily Bible reading notes which follow the Church of England's weekday Lectionary – *Reflections for Daily Prayer* (Church House Publishing, published annually). See www.dailyprayer.org.uk.

Where to find the Weekday Lectionary

The Weekday Lectionary is not published in any of the main *Common Worship* volumes. If you want to start from scratch, you can download the undated Weekday Lectionary tables from the Church of England website and then work out what the readings are for particular dates in the current year – but that's a lot of hard work and gets very complicated once you start taking account of saints' days and how the date of Easter affects the rest of the year. It's usually a lot easier to use one of the following:

- The *Common Worship Lectionary* booklet is published each year by Church House Publishing. This gives the readings for each day of the year (including Sundays). The booklet starts on Advent Sunday and runs through to the eve of Advent the following year. Someone else does all the hard work, and all you have to do is find the right date. It also gives guidance about the appropriate liturgical colour for each day of the year.
- The same annual Lectionary booklet can also be purchased as an electronic download from the Church House Publishing website. It is available in two forms: either as a simple table which can be viewed using spreadsheet software on your computer or in a

format that can be imported into an electronic calendar or diary. See the website for more information: www.chpublishing.co.uk.

- The Lectionary published annually by SPCK in a booklet form is a similar resource, which gives *Book of Common Prayer* Lectionary readings as well as *Common Worship*.
- *The Order for the Eucharist and for Morning and Evening Prayer* (commonly known as 'The Ordo') is produced annually by John Hunwicke and published by Tufton Books. This includes Calendar and Lectionary information from the Roman Catholic Church as well as for the Church of England.
- Many diaries produced for church use also include the Lectionary for each day. Examples include: The *Canterbury Church Book and Desk Diary* (Norwich Canterbury Press; *CW* and *BCP*), which is also available in loose-leaf format for either a standard or A5-size personal organizer; the *Church Pocket Book and Diary* (London: SPCK: *CW* only); *The Parson's Pocket Book* (Atkinsons: *CW* only).

The Additional Weekday Lectionary

The first version of the *Common Worship* Weekday Lectionary took a different approach from the one outlined in this section. One aspect of this different approach has lived on in the Additional Weekday Lectionary (sometimes referred to as the 'pillar' lectionary), which was given Final Approval by General Synod in July 2010 and will be published as a downloadable PDF document.

This is a daily Lectionary for one service per day, which uses readings which might connect with one another and which 'stand alone', rather than following on from the previous day. This is designed for situations where the congregation is not constant from day to day, such as cathedral Evensong services, or churches with a pattern of Morning or Evening Prayer which does not happen every day or which happens at different times on different days.

Quick Tip: Lectionary for Night Prayer

There is no daily lectionary for Night Prayer. Instead, use the form provided in *Common Worship: Daily Prayer*, which gives suggested psalms and short readings which can be varied daily and seasonally.

The Psalms in the Weekday Lectionary

The psalms appointed for each day work differently depending on what time of year it is.

Seasonal Time	*Ordinary Time*
The psalms for each day are chosen from a selection of psalms which are appropriate to the season. Alternatively, you can follow the sequential pattern from Ordinary Time.	The psalms are basically appointed sequentially (that is, working through from Psalm 1 to Psalm 150) across both Morning and Evening Prayer (for example, Psalms 41, 42 and 43 in the morning and Psalms 44 and 46 in the evening).

N.B. The 'sequential' pattern is not *strictly* sequential because psalms are appointed to the appropriate time of day (for example, a psalm about the sunrise is not used for Evening Prayer) and those which are selected for the seasons are used less in Ordinary Time.

Quick Tip: Choosing from a selection of psalms

On most days, the Lectionary gives more than one psalm for each service. If you want only one psalm, the one printed in bold print in the Lectionary is the one to go for.

For more on *Common Worship: Daily Prayer*, see below, Chapter 7, p. 109.

For more on the Psalms in *Common Worship*, see below, Chapter 8, p. 116.

The Collects

What is a collect?

A collect is a prayer with a particular structure.

Elements of a Collect	Example (*CW*, 3rd Sunday of Easter)
An **address** to God.	*Almighty Father,*
A **truth** about God, which may be the basis for asking.	*who in your great mercy gladdened the disciples with the sight of the risen Lord:*
A **request**, sometimes based on this truth.	*give us such knowledge of his presence with us,*
[Sometimes the **purpose** of that request is spelled out.]	*that we may be strengthened and sustained by his risen life and serve you continually in righteousness and truth;*
The **conclusion**, giving the authority for asking, and possibly concluding with a Trinitarian formula.	*through Jesus Christ your Son our Lord, who is alive and reigns with you, in the unity of the Holy Spirit, one God, now and for ever.*

From Mark Earey, *Liturgical Worship* (London: Church House Publishing, 2002), p. 83.

Collect prayers are designed to 'collect together' the prayers of the people (which may have been silent or spoken). In a Communion service the collect usually comes at the conclusion of the Gathering section of the service (gathering the prayers of everyone and focusing them before the move into the Liturgy of the Word).

Quick Tip: How to use the collect

Note that the rubric stresses the importance of the silence after the introduction, before the president leads the collect itself (main volume, p. 171). This is to make sure that the people have a chance to pray their own prayers, before they are 'gathered' by the president in the words of the collect.

Sometimes the Collect of the Day can be used to conclude a section of prayers, such as prayers of intercession. Another pattern is for collect-style prayers to form the basis of the prayers, with a collect-style prayer concluding each section of biddings or silence. The Prayer Book services of Morning and Evening Prayer conclude the service with a series of collects, including the Collect of the Day.

The *BCP* set a Church of England pattern of using the Sunday collect as a 'prayer of the week', holding together the prayers of clergy and lay people between Sundays. *Common Worship* follows this pattern, providing a Collect prayer for each Sunday (which may be used on the following weekdays) and for all the main feasts and festivals of the church year (such as saints' days, Christmas, Ascension, Ash Wednesday, etc.). In addition, *Common Worship: Daily Prayer* provides collects at Morning and Evening Prayer for each day of the week in Ordinary Time and for each season of the year.

Three sets of Collects

There are three sets of *Common Worship* Collects.

- The original *Common Worship* Collects in contemporary language.
- The original *Common Worship* Collects in traditional language.
- A set of Additional Collects, which were published in 2005.

Quick Tip: Know how to use your endings

The *Common Worship* Collects are printed with the full Trinitarian ending (typically, 'through Jesus Christ your Son our Lord, who is alive and reigns with you, in the unity of the Holy Spirit, one God, now and for ever'). This makes them feel longer than they need to. Note 5 on p. 375 makes clear that a shorter ending ('through Jesus Christ our Lord') can replace this, though it suggests the longer ending might be 'preferred' at Holy Communion.

FAQ – Where do the *Common Worship* Collects come from?

Many of the *Common Worship* Collects and some of the Post Communions are based on originals in the *Book of Common Prayer*. Others are drawn from other sources, including the service books of other parts of the Anglican Communion. There are two places to look for information on the sources of the *Common Worship* Collects and Post Communions:

- There is a table in the main volume (pp. 522–3) which tells you which *Common Worship* Collects and Post

Communions for Sundays and Festivals are based on Prayer
Book originals, and what those originals are.
- For a more thorough list of the sources of all the Collects
and Post Communions, see *Common Worship: Collects and
Post Communions*, pp. 181–5.

The **Additional Collects** are generally shorter and simpler in construction
(designed to be written in a 'worthy contemporary idiom') and use more
creative images.

Quick Tip: Collects for a season: know your asterisks

In the set of Additional Collects, some are marked with a double
asterisk (**). A collect which is designated in this way can replace
the Collect of the Day on any other day in the same season. For
Ordinary Time there is more than one collect marked like this. This
means that you could choose to use a collect consistently through a
season or a period of Ordinary Time, encouraging a congregation to
learn it by heart and use it at home too.

Where to find the Collects

- *Common Worship* Collects in contemporary language begin on p.
375 in the main volume. They are also printed in the *President's
Edition*, in *Common Worship Times and Seasons: President's
Edition for Holy Communion*, and in *Common Worship: Daily
Prayer*.
- *Common Worship* Collects in traditional language begin on p. 448
in the main volume. They are printed in the *President's Edition* and
can also be found in a large format booklet *Common Worship:
Collects and Post-Communions in Traditional Language*.
- The Additional Collects can be found in a large format booklet,
Common Worship: Additional Collects.
- Extra Collects, for Lesser Festivals, special occasions and 'Common
of the Saints' (that is, non-specific Collects for different types of
saints, such as martyrs, bishops, etc.) can be found in *Common
Worship: Festivals* and in *Common Worship: Daily Prayer*.

- The *Common Worship: Collects and Post-Communions* volume includes both the modern and traditional sets of collects (including for Lesser Festivals etc.), plus the Additional Collects.
- Don't forget – all the Collects (including the Additional set) can be downloaded from the Church of England website. See above, p. 3, for details.

Quick Tip: Liturgical colours

The collects section in the *Common Worship* main volume is also a good place to look if you aren't sure about the liturgical colour – the colour is indicated in red next to each Sunday or Festival heading.

FAQ – Why do some of the 'contemporary' *Common Worship* Collects sound old-fashioned?

Where *Common Worship* Collects have been derived from those in the *BCP*, the modern versions have been designed to echo the Prayer Book original as much as possible. This is one of the factors which led to the production of the set of Additional Collects, designed to be less 'old-fashioned' in style.

Quick Tip: Getting the Collect in the right language version

If you are using Collect prayers from the *Common Worship* main volume, make sure your marker is in the right section (that is, contemporary or traditional language). Because the traditional set follows the contemporary set, it's easy to get the wrong ones if you open the book and search quickly for the Sunday or Festival that you want.

FAQ – Do we have to use the 'official' *Common Worship* Collects?

The Collects are an authorized set of texts, alternative to those in the *Book of Common Prayer* (see p. 15, above). The rubric in Holy Communion Order One simply says, 'The Collect is said . . . ', assuming one of the authorized texts. A Service of the Word with a Celebration of Holy Communion (main volume, p. 25) makes it clear: the Collect is one of the few items marked with an asterisk, indicating that an authorized text must be used. However, the introduction to A Service of the Word (main volume, p. 22) specifically says that the Collect does not have to be the Collect of the Day, but could be a thematic one based on the readings. This presumably allows for a locally composed text or one from a non-authorized source.

In short, there is a strong steer towards using one of the authorized texts, for the sake of commonality across the Church of England, but Canon B 5's permission for changes which are not of substantial importance probably gives leeway for others to be used (see 'Can I change the words', p. 18, for more on Canon B 5). If you are going to write a collect for a particular theme, situation or service, there is good guidance in *New Patterns for Worship* on p. 176. For more general advice on constructing prayers and texts for worship, see Ruth Duck, *Finding Words for Worship: A Guide for Leaders* (Louisville, K Y: Westminster John Knox Press, 1995).

How the Collects relate to the readings

Collects are linked to named Sundays (for example, the Collect of Advent Sunday) and not to Bible readings. This means that the Collects do not, generally, work as 'theme' prayers for each Sunday, though in the seasons they will have a strong thematic link with the season itself.

In Seasonal Time, this is straightforward: you simply find the readings and Collect for the particular Sunday or Festival.

In Ordinary Time things get more complicated.

- The Collects are still linked to the Sunday titles (for example, the Second Sunday after Trinity).

- The readings are connected to the date. Sets of readings in Ordinary Time are called 'Propers' – that is, 'appropriate' to a particular date (for example, Proper 12 is the set of readings for the Sunday between 17 and 23 July).

FAQ – Why don't the Collects connect with the readings?

The Collects work on a one-year cycle, related to the Sundays of the year, rather than a three-year cycle like the readings in the Lectionary.

This was out of a hope that the Collects would become well known (perhaps even known by heart, as folk-memory suggests the Prayer Book Collects often were in previous generations) because they came round every year. This hope was rather deflated by the authorization of the set of Additional Collects, which acknowledged that the 'one-size-fits-all' approach would not work, and that a choice of collect prayer which was right for the particular context was more appropriate.

If you are looking for sets of collects that do connect with the readings of the three-year lectionary, then you could try *Opening Prayers: Scripture-related Collects for Years A, B & C from The Sacramentary* (Norwich: Canterbury Press, 1999) or Steven Shakespeare, *Prayers for an Inclusive Church* (Norwich: Canterbury Press, 2008).

Post Communion Prayers

Common Worship provides a Post Communion Prayer for each Sunday and Festival. These are designed to be said by the president. They are intended to *precede* (not replace) the congregational Post Communion Prayer (typically, either 'Father of all, we give you thanks and praise . . . ' or 'Almighty God, we thank you for feeding us . . . ' – see the *Common Worship* main volume, p. 182). There are additional Post Communions for president and for congregation in *New Patterns for Worship*, pp. 297–300. See also *Common Worship: Festivals*.

Further reading for this chapter

Horace Allen and Joseph Russell, *On Common Ground: The Story of the Revised Common Lectionary*, Norwich: Canterbury Press, 1998.

Gill Ambrose, *Together for a Season*, London: Church House Publishing 2006, 2007 and 2009 respectively (three volumes of all-age resources covering Advent, Christmas and Epiphany; Lent, Holy Week and Easter; and Feasts and Festivals of the Christian Year).

Paul Bradshaw (ed.), *A Companion to Common Worship – Vol. 1*, London: SPCK, 2001, Chapters 8 and 9; and *A Companion to Common Worship – Vol. 2*, London: SPCK, 2006, Chapters 2 and 5.

Colin Buchanan, Mark Earey, Gilly Myers and Tim Stratford, *Collects: An Alternative View*, Grove Worship Series No. 171, Cambridge: Grove Books, 2002.

Mark Earey, *How to Choose Songs and Hymns for Worship*, Grove Worship Series 201, Cambridge: Grove Books, 2009.

Mark Earey, Trevor Lloyd, Peter Moger and Tim Stratford, *Introducing Times and Season 1: The Christmas Cycle*, Grove Worship Series No. 189, Cambridge: Grove Books, 2006.

Mark Earey and Gilly Myers (eds), *Common Worship Today – Study Edition*, Nottingham: St John's Extension Studies, 2007, Chapter 14.

Benjamin Gordon-Taylor and Simon Jones, *Celebrating Christ's Appearing: Advent to Candlemas*, Alcuin Liturgy Guides No. 5, London: SPCK, 2008; and *Celebrating Christ's Victory: Ash Wednesday to Trinity*, Alcuin Liturgy Guides No. 6, London: SPCK, 2008.

David Kennedy, *Using Common Worship: Times and Seasons Volume 1 – All Saints to Candlemas*, London: Church House Publishing, 2006.

David Kennedy with Jeremy Haselock, *Using Common Worship: Times and Seasons Volume 2 – Lent to Embertide*, London: Church House Publishing, 2008.

Trevor Lloyd, Peter Moger, Jane Sinclair and Michael Vasey, *Introducing the New Lectionary*, Grove Worship Series No. 141, Cambridge: Grove Books, 1997.

Michael Perham, *Celebrate the Christian Story*, London: SPCK, 1997.

Michael Perham, *New Handbook of Pastoral Liturgy*, London: SPCK, 2000, Chapters 7, 9, 10, 12 and 29–34.

Phillip Tovey (ed.), *Introducing Times and Seasons 2: The Easter Cycle*, Grove Worship Series No. 190, Cambridge: Grove Books, 2007.

3

Services of the Word

What is 'A Service of the Word'?

A Service of the Word is the 'authorized alternative' to Morning and Evening Prayer in the *Book of Common Prayer*. It can be used in several ways:

- As the framework for non-Eucharistic services on Sundays (for example, all-age services, morning or evening worship, youth services, etc.).
- As a framework for Daily Prayer.
- As the framework for Holy Communion – see *Common Worship*, main volume, p. 25 or *NPW*, p. 12.

A Service of the Word does not lay down any particular shape or structure. *New Patterns for Worship*, for instance, offers two possible ways of structuring a service:

- A 'block' structure – *NPW*, p. 18.
- A 'conversation' structure – *NPW*, p. 19. This consists of several 'word' elements, each of which has an element of response. This is similar to Morning and Evening Prayer in the *BCP*.

Other ways of structuring services are possible and, indeed, encouraged – the key thing being that there *is* a clear structure and that this has been given some thought so that there is integrity between the content of the service and the way it is structured.

Where to find A Service of the Word

It is printed in two places:

- *Common Worship* main volume, pp. 21–7.
- *New Patterns for Worship*, pp. 9–14.

Although the Service of the Word itself is a fairly short list of items, it is vital to read carefully the introductory material which precedes it and the Notes that follow, in order to get the full picture.

A Service of the Word is printed in *New Patterns for Worship* because the resource material (and the way the book is arranged) is ideally suited to it, but other material can be used as well.

Understanding the limits and the scope

A Service of the Word assigns different levels of importance to different elements of the service:

- Some elements are **compulsory** (such as the use of the Lord's Prayer).
- Some elements are **recommended** but not compulsory (such as the use of canticles or a set of responses).
- Other elements are **optional** and may be added at the discretion of the local leaders (for example, hymns or songs).

Whether an element is compulsory or not also depends on whether the service is a Sunday service or a weekday service (see table below).

There are also differences in the amount of choice allowed for each element:

- Sometimes there is **wide scope** (for instance, the form of intercession used). The only constraint is that which applies to all services, that they should be appropriate for public worship and consistent with Church of England doctrine.
- Sometimes there is **limited scope** (for instance, there are a limited number of authorized confessions and absolutions).

The notes encourage the use of silence during the service and suggest points at which this may be particularly appropriate. The notes also make clear that the use of songs or hymns at various points in the service is a matter for local decision.

> **Quick Tip: The quickest way to find all the options**
>
> The quickest and easiest way to find the full range of authorized texts for Confessions and Creeds and Affirmations of Faith is to look in *New Patterns for Worship*, Sections B and E respectively.

What do you have to include?

The table below summarizes the situation. A '•' in the column means it must be included; brackets indicate that there may be exceptions.

Element of A Service of the Word	Principal Service on Sunday	Other Sunday Service	Daily Prayer
Greeting (*this should include a 'liturgical greeting' of some sort*)	•	•	•
Authorized **Prayers of Penitence** (*See* New Patterns for Worship, *Section B, for all the authorized options*)	•		
Venite, Gloria, Kyries, a hymn, song or set of responses may be used			
The **Collect** (*This does not necessarily mean the Collect of the Day*)	•	•	•
Readings from Scripture (*Two, or at the very least, one*)	•	•	•
Psalm (*Or other scriptural or psalm-based hymn or song should 'normally' be included*)	(•)	(•)	(•)
Sermon	•	•	
Authorized **Creed** or **Affirmation of Faith** (*See* New Patterns for Worship, *Section E, for all the authorized options*)	•		

49

Intercessions and thanksgivings	•	•	•
The Lord's Prayer	•	•	•
Clear ending – the Peace, the Grace, or a suitable ascription or blessing	•	•	•

For more detail on the particular permissions and restrictions, see the Notes which accompany A Service of the Word and the Introduction to the section (main volume, pp. 21–3 and pp. 26–7 respectively, and the equivalent pages in *NPW*).

Note that the term 'sermon' is not meant to be restricted to a traditional monologue, but includes 'less formal exposition, the use of drama, interviews, discussion, audio-visuals and the insertion of hymns or other sections of the service between parts of the sermon' (Note 7 from A Service of the Word).

FAQ – Where is the *Common Worship* All-Age (or Family) service?

There is no specific *Common Worship* All-Age Service. Such services are covered by A Service of the Word, so the key is to be creative and draw on resources from suitable sources (including specialist resources for inter-generational worship), while using the Service of the Word structure to keep an eye on content. *New Patterns for Worship* has a range of resources, and also some sample services which may give some ideas.

Further reading for this chapter

Paul Bradshaw (ed.), *A Companion to Common Worship – Vol. 1*, London: SPCK, 2001, Chapter 4.

Mark Earey and Gilly Myers (eds), *Common Worship Today – Study Edition*, Nottingham: St John's Extension Studies, 2007, Chapter 10.

Michael Perham, *New Handbook of Pastoral Liturgy*, London: SPCK, 2000, Chapters 19 and 21.

Tim Stratford, *Using Common Worship: A Service of the Word*, London: Church House Publishing, 2002.

4

Holy Communion

The different structures for Communion

There are three basic structures for Communion services in *Common Worship*:

- Order One – in two language forms.
- Order Two – in two language forms.
- A Service of the Word with a Celebration of Holy Communion – an outline order.

Order One

This follows the standard 'modern ecumenical' shape for a Eucharist (with scope for variation – see the Notes). The four main section headings (The Gathering; The Liturgy of the Word; The Liturgy of the Sacrament; The Dismissal) reflect this.

The default is a contemporary language service, but there is also a traditional language version. The traditional language form follows the structure of Order One, but has a few differences in the detail of the text:

- Only the Prayer Book form of Humble Access is given.
- There is a choice of only two Eucharistic Prayers (A and C).
- The Prayer of Oblation from the Prayer Book is an alternative to the Post Communion, and there is no alternative to the congregational prayer, 'Almighty God, we thank thee for feeding us . . . ' (in other words, the prayer, 'Father of all . . . ' is not offered in a traditional language form).

Order Two

This follows the structure of the 1662 Prayer Book Communion service (so, for instance, it begins with the Commandments, and the *Gloria in excelsis* comes at the end). This makes Order Two effectively the Prayer Book Communion service 'as used' (that is, with the customary variations commonly used in many churches). The 'customary variations' from the pattern of the Prayer Book are indicated by indented text (for example, replacing the Ten Commandments with the commandments of Jesus and using a congregational response before and after the Gospel Reading).

The default is a traditional language service, but there is also a contemporary language version. There are more detailed differences between Order Two and Order Two (Contemporary) than between the two versions of Order One, but the basic structure is again the same.

A Service of the Word with Holy Communion

This is a basic outline order, like A Service of the Word, and so the actual texts used in the service could be contemporary or traditional or a mixture of both. Read the accompanying Notes carefully, especially Note 10: 'The order provided is not prescriptive' (*Common Worship*, main volume, p. 27). See also the introductory rubric on p. 25, 'This rite . . . is not normally to be used as the regular Sunday or weekday service.'

Where to find the Holy Communion services

The main volume is the place to look, though Order One and Order Two can also be found in the *President's Edition*, and Order One is printed in *Common Worship: Festivals* and in *Common Worship Times and Seasons: President's Edition for Holy Communion* and *Common Worship: Holy Week and Easter.*

In the main volume:

- Order One starts on p. 167. The traditional language version begins on p. 207.
- Order Two starts on p. 229. The contemporary language version begins on p. 249.
- A Service of the Word with Holy Communion is on p. 25 in the main volume, but can also be found on p. 12 in *New Patterns for Worship.*

Quick Tip: Get to know the Notes

The Notes to the Communion services are on pp. 330–5 in the main volume, separated from the actual services by pages and pages of supplementary material. They give useful information about what flexibility is allowed.

FAQ – What is the simplest form of Communion service?

The most obviously 'minimalist' version of Holy Communion provided in *Common Worship* is *A Service of the Word with Holy Communion*.

There is a lot of flexibility (for example, it doesn't necessarily have to follow the order in which it is printed in the book) and the only texts specified are that the Confession, the Collect and the Eucharistic Prayer must use authorized forms. There are other requirements too (for example, there must be Scripture readings and prayers for the Church and the world) but there are no fixed words associated with these.

Users need to note that the service is preceded by a rubric that says it is 'not normally' to be used as the regular Sunday service, but in actual fact a careful reading of Order One with its notes and rubrics reveals that there's almost as much flexibility built into that anyway.

Quick Tip: Lighter typeface options

In Order One, you might notice that some texts look as if they are printed in lighter typeface. This is deliberate, and occurs when General Synod decided that some texts should be given 'more weight' within a range of options (or, in effect, other texts should be given less weight). For examples, see the opening Trinitarian ascription on p. 167 and the words at the Breaking of the Bread on p. 179 in the main volume. In the latter case, the first option ('We break this bread to share in the body of Christ . . . ') is given 'more weight' than the second ('Every time we eat this bread and drink this cup . . . '). See the second rubric at the start of the Notes on p. 330 in the main volume for the official explanation of the lighter typeface.

Seasonal material in the main volume

If you are leading a service of Holy Communion from the main volume, you will find very little seasonal material there. There are some 'propers' for the president to use (see the Seasonal Provisions, starting on p. 300, and some parts of the Supplementary Texts, starting on p. 268).

However, don't forget that there are some variable texts for the congregation too, hidden away in the supplementary texts for Holy Communion and in the Service of the Word section of the book:

- The Summary of the Law and the Ten Commandments (pp. 268–71).
- Confessions (pp. 123–34 and pp. 276–8).
- Creeds and Affirmations of Faith (pp. 139–48).
- Prayers at the Preparation of the Table (pp. 291–3).
- Congregational Prayers after Communion (p. 297).

A Form of Preparation

Printed before the main orders for Holy Communion (and therefore often overlooked) is A Form of Preparation (main volume, pp. 161–5). This can be used as a separate short act of preparation by individuals before the service (either at home or in church) or it could be used corporately. It can also be used on occasion as a replacement for the Prayer of Preparation and the Prayers of Penitence in the Order One Holy Communion service itself. In particular, it includes a short exhortation, phrased slightly differently from the version on p. 274 in the Supplementary Texts (and included in Order Two in contemporary language).

Quick Tip: Page numbers in the red booklet

If you are leading a Communion service and the congregation (or at least some of them) are using the red Order One booklets (or the blue Order Two booklets), it's worth knowing that there is double-page numbering in the booklets. The numbers on the outer edge of each page give the booklet page number (that is, starting at p. 1). Towards the inner edge of each page there is another set of page numbers, which match the page numbering of the main volume. This is very useful if some of the congregation are using the booklets, but others are using the main volume. This situation might occur, for instance, if a church has bought a relatively small number of copies of the main volume, supplemented by extra booklets when there is a larger congregation. In such a case, the president can direct people by giving just one set of page numbers – those of the main volume – as long as it is explained clearly to the booklet users.

The *President's Edition* also has double page numbering, so that the president can give numbers which match the main volume.

FAQ – Where should we put the notices?

Note 9 to the Holy Communion services (main volume, p. 331) suggests three possible positions for the notices:

- before the Gathering;
- before the Intercessions;
- before the Dismissal.

New Patterns for Worship gives more detailed advice on p. 31.

The Greeting

Note the order of texts at the very start of the service:

- The Trinitarian ascription ('In the name of the Father . . . ') is optional.
- The greeting proper begins with 'The Lord be with you' (or the fuller alternative).

- Then, in the Easter season, the Easter acclamation ('Alleluia. Christ is risen . . . ') comes as a *supplement* to the greeting (not an alternative).
- Then (and only then) the rubric suggests more informal words of welcome or introduction.

Quick Tip: More than one place for penitence

The Prayers of Penitence are printed in only one position in the Holy Communion service, but the Notes specifically mention that they could be transposed to a different position (for instance, later in the service as part of the response to the sermon). See Note 10, main volume, p. 331.

Gospel Acclamations

In Order One and Order Two (Contemporary Language) the rubric mentions that, 'An acclamation may herald the Gospel reading.' This refers to Alleluia acclamations, which are an optional addition to the normal announcement of the Gospel ('Hear the Gospel of our Lord Jesus Christ . . . '). Suitable acclamations for Ordinary Time can be found in the main volume on p. 280, and further suggestions are found in the Seasonal Provisions starting on p. 300, but others can be devised drawing from appropriate passages of Scripture. Note that in Lent the suggested acclamation avoids the use of Alleluia, in keeping with the common Lenten tradition.

Quick Tip: Announcing the Gospel reading

Note 12 (main volume, p. 332) suggests that if the reading is to be announced with chapter and verse or page number, this may be done informally first, before saying, 'Hear the gospel of our Lord Jesus Christ according to *N*'. If you try to tack the verse or page number information on the end of the formal announcement, it can sound rather clumsy, and the congregation become less sure when to come in with their response.

FAQ – Is a Gospel reading required at Holy Communion?

Yes. *Common Worship* recognizes that a service of Holy Communion might include the full three readings (Old Testament, New Testament and Gospel) or just two. In the latter case, one of the two should be a Gospel reading (see the rubrics in the Holy Communion services, and Rule 6 on p. 540 of the main volume).

Credal options

Although the Nicene Creed is printed in the text of the Holy Communion services and is the 'norm', there other possibilities, most of which can be found in the Supplementary Texts which follow A Service of the Word in the main volume (pp. 138–48), or in Section E of *New Patterns for Worship*. The other possibilities are:

- The Nicene Creed in a responsorial form.
- The Apostles' Creed, in either contemporary or traditional forms, or in a question-and-answer format.
- One of the authorized Affirmations of Faith. On p. 159 of *New Patterns for Worship* there are suggestions about which Affirmations to use in different seasons. Don't forget that one of the authorized Affirmations is a metrical version which can be sung to several well-known hymn tunes.
- The Athanasian Creed, which is printed in full only in the *Book of Common Prayer*. Note that one of the Affirmations of Faith is based on part of the Athanasian Creed.
- A version of the Nicene Creed in the main volume (p. 140) for use 'on suitable ecumenical occasions'. This version has 'who proceeds from the Father' (omitting 'and the Son', the so-called 'filioque' clause). This makes it particularly appropriate to use when Christians of the Orthodox Churches are present.

Eucharistic Prayers

The number of Eucharistic Prayers varies across the four main versions of the Communion service:

	Order One	**Order One** (traditional)	**Order Two**	**Order Two** (contemporary)
Eucharistic Prayers	Eight prayers (A, B, C, D, E, F, G, H)	Two prayers (A, C)	One prayer, built into the service on the Prayer Book model	One prayer, built into the service on the Prayer Book model, in contemporary language

Eucharistic Prayers, Proper Prefaces and congregational responses

Common Worship allows for two main ways of making the Eucharistic Prayer seasonal, or appropriate to the theme of the service:

- Short Proper Prefaces – these are added to the end of the praise section of the prayer between the opening dialogue and the Sanctus.
- Extended Prefaces – these *replace* the whole of the praise section of the prayer between the opening dialogue and the Sanctus.

You can find short and extended prefaces in the main volume (p. 294 for Ordinary Time and pp. 300–29 for Seasons) and in *Common Worship: Times and Seasons* and *Common Worship: Festivals*.

Not all the Eucharistic Prayers are designed to work with these prefaces – see the table below. The table also shows which prayers have congregational responses (in addition to the opening dialogue, the Sanctus, and the memorial acclamations). In the table, brackets indicate optional material.

	A	**B**	**C**	**D**	**E**	**F**	**G**	**H**
Short preface?	•	•	•					
Extended preface?	•	•			•			
Congregational responses?	(•)			•		(•)		•

Note that this means that in prayers D, F, G and H there is no scope for seasonal variation.

See also Note 18 on p. 333 in the main volume for more detail on how to use the prefaces with the prayers.

Short prefaces can also be used with the consecration prayer in Order Two, but the phrasing of the prayer needs to be altered slightly (see Note 28 on p. 335 in the main volume).

Length of Eucharistic Prayers

Figure 2 shows the relative length of each Eucharistic Prayer (assuming there are no extra or extended prefaces and the choice of memorial acclamation is the same). Choosing a prayer according to how long it is may not usually be the most appropriate criterion, but sometimes it is helpful to recognize the impact of a choice of prayer. In the chart, Prayers A and F are shown including the optional responses; the dotted line indicates the length of the prayer omitting those responses.

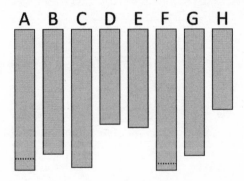

Figure 2: The relative lengths of the Eucharistic Prayers in Order One

FAQ – Why are the Eucharistic Prayers printed after the service?

The eight Eucharistic Prayers of Order One are printed in full at the end of the service, rather than at the point at which the Eucharistic Prayer occurs. At that point there is instead a two-page spread which gives just the congregational responses required for all the prayers. The thinking behind this was to make the service flow more easily in the book, without requiring the congregation to skip over several pages. It had the additional effect of encouraging the congregation to look up and follow the action, rather than following the text in the book. It made some sense when there were seven

Eucharistic Prayers with fairly regular congregational responses, but when Prayer H was added at the last moment, the idea rather lost its advantage, because Prayer H has to be followed in full because the congregational part varies through the prayer.

Quick Tip: Producing your own prefaces

New Patterns for Worship, section G, contains a number of short prefaces (pp. 258–67) and a wide range of Thanksgivings (pp. 234–57) which can be adapted to make extended prefaces, including many with congregational responses. There is advice about how to use these, and on producing your own prefaces, on p. 222.

FAQ – Which Eucharistic Prayer is best for all-age services?

None of the prayers in *Common Worship* was specifically designated as all-age friendly, but some work better than others. The temptation is to opt for the shortest prayer (Prayer H), but this does not work well for young children (or others) who cannot read, because the congregational responses are all different from one another. Prayer E in its basic form is quite short and so is Prayer D. Prayer D has the added advantage of a consistent response which can be memorized. Rather than going for a short prayer, it may be better to choose a prayer which has responses which can be learned by heart, or, even better, sung by heart.

Eucharistic Prayers for use when a large number of children are present are currently making their way through the General Synod authorization process, and may provide more options (particularly for school Eucharists). The fact that these are designed for when large numbers of children are present, however, does not necessarily make them good choices for all-age services, where the congregation includes, but is not dominated by, children.

Quick Tip: Supplementary consecration

If either the consecrated bread or wine runs out, you'll need the words for supplementary consecration, which are on p. 296 of the main volume.

FAQ – Is there a special form of words for blessing non-communicants?

When children or adults who are not yet confirmed or admitted to Communion come forward with others at the time of distribution of Communion, it is the practice in most churches to offer a 'prayer of blessing'. A suggested form of words can be found in the main volume in Note 21, p. 334: 'May God be with you', or 'May God bless you'. These words, in the form of a prayer rather than a declaration, are appropriate for lay or ordained people to use.

A discussion paper by the Liturgical Commission ('Prayer for Non-Communicants', 2007) clarifies some of the theological and liturgical issues and gives slightly more detailed guidance. It recommends accompanying the words with a formalized gesture, which might include laying a hand on the head of a child or on the shoulder of an adult. It also recommends that the person administering the bread be the one to offer the prayer, and that it not be repeated or supplemented by the person administering the wine. The Commission also suggests words which are more specifically Christ-focused as being appropriate for the Communion context:

'May Christ who welcomes you give you his blessing.'
'May Christ fill you with his life and his love.'
'May the Lord Jesus bless you and keep you' – particularly for infants and young children.

The discussion paper can be downloaded from the Transforming Worship website: www.transformingworship.org.uk. Click on 'Papers from the Liturgical Commission' and download it from there.

After Communion

The rubric in Order One mentions a Post Communion and then has a rubric, 'All may say one of these prayers', before printing two congregational prayers.

The 'Post Communion' mentioned first means one of the presidential texts, provided along with Collects for each Sunday, Feast, Festival and Holy Day. Though the rubric suggests this is compulsory, Note 22 (main volume, p. 334) gives three options:

- A presidential prayer only (normally the Post Communion of the day).
- One of the congregational prayers only.
- A presidential prayer and one congregational prayer.

Communion by Extension

Communion by Extension (sometimes referred to as 'extended Communion') is a Communion service using bread and wine that have previously been consecrated, either at the same church (for example, at an earlier service) or at a church somewhere else (for example, another church in the benefice, team or deanery).

Its full title is 'Public Worship with Communion by Extension', and it is not, technically, a *Common Worship* service, though the two forms of service it provides are deliberately based on *Common Worship* Order One and Order Two.

Where to find Communion by Extension

Public Worship with Communion by Extension was published by CHP in 2001. It can be downloaded from the Church of England website along with the *Common Worship* resources (see above, p. 3, for details).

When can we use it?

It is intended for occasional use to cover emergency or unusual circumstances (for example, the illness of a priest, or provision during a vacancy in the parish or clergy holidays). It is not intended to be the normal diet of Holy Communion services for any congregation or parish.

It is also not intended to be used for Communion services with the sick or housebound – for those situations, see *Common Worship: Pastoral Services* (more information in Chapter 6).

Who can lead Communion by Extension?

The service can be led by a deacon or a Reader, or by another lay person *specifically* authorized to do so by the bishop. Those who are authorized to help with the distribution of Holy Communion are *not* automatically authorized to *lead* one of these services without further training and specific authorization from the bishop.

What printed words do we need?

Many churches will print their own order of service for extended Communion, but as a one-off or in an emergency it can be led almost entirely using congregational texts from a *Common Worship* main volume (or locally produced Holy Communion booklet). The leader will need the full text of *Public Worship with Communion by Extension*, but the only words that the congregation need which are not in the main volume are the words for the prayer, 'Blessed are you, God of those who hunger and thirst . . .', which comes immediately before the Lord's Prayer, preceding the distribution of Communion.

Further reading for this chapter

Mark Beach, *Using Common Worship: Holy Communion*, London: Church House Publishing, 2000.

Paul Bradshaw (ed.), *A Companion to Common Worship – Vol. 1*, London: SPCK, 2001, pp. 98–108.

Colin Buchanan and Charles Read, *The Eucharistic Prayers of Order One*, Grove Worship Series 158, Cambridge: Grove Books, 2000.

Stephen Burns, *Living the Thanksgiving: Exploring the Eucharist*, London: Canterbury Press, 2006 – a booklet for parish study.

Mark Earey and Gilly Myers (eds), *Common Worship Today – Study Edition*, Nottingham: St John's Extension Studies, 2007, Chapter 9.

Jeremy Fletcher, *Communion in Common Worship: The Shape of Orders One and Two*, Grove Worship Series 159, Cambridge: Grove Books, 2000.

Benjamin Gordon-Taylor and Simon Jones, *Celebrating the Eucharist*, Alcuin Liturgy Guides 3, London: SPCK, 2005.

Michael Perham, *New Handbook of Pastoral Liturgy*, London: SPCK, 2000, Chapters 14–18.

Kenneth Stevenson, *Do This: The Shape, Style and Meaning of the Eucharist*, Norwich: Canterbury Press, 2002.

Communion by extension

Paul Bradshaw (ed.), *A Companion to Common Worship – Vol. 2*, London: SPCK, 2006, Chapter 11.

Phillip Tovey, *Public Worship with Communion by Extension: A Commentary*, Grove Worship Series 167, Cambridge: Grove Books, 2001.

5

Initiation Services

Where to find the *Common Worship* initiation services

The obvious and central place to look is the *Common Worship: Christian Initiation* volume itself, where all the services are printed. However, some services crop up in other places too:

- The basic version of the baptism service is also printed in the *Common Worship* main volume (pp. 344ff.). This is useful if you are leading a main Sunday service which includes a baptism, and the congregation has the main volume. The basic Baptism Service is also reproduced in the *President's Edition*.
- The Thanksgiving for the Gift of a Child service is also printed in the *Common Worship* main volume (pp. 337ff.) and in *Common Worship: Pastoral Services* (pp. 200ff.).

Quick Tip: The preliminary edition – *Common Worship: Initiation Services*, 1998

Watch out for *Common Worship: Initiation Services*, London: Church House Publishing, 1998. This was the first edition of the *Common Worship* initiation services, still in use by some clergy but now out of date (the rubrics have since been loosened up, making more things optional). This earlier volume also does not have the 'Rites on the Way' and reconciliation material. It is useful, however, because it includes fully printed out versions of complicated things like Baptism with Confirmation and Affirmation of Baptismal Faith in a Eucharist, which are only covered by complicated tables in the later *Common Worship: Christian Initiation* volume.

What's in the package?

Common Worship: Christian Initiation includes a lot more than just the Baptism and Confirmation Services.

There are basically four sections:

Rites on the Way: Approaching Baptism

- Thanksgiving for the Gift of a Child.
- Rites supporting disciples on the Way of Christ – that is, material to use alongside evangelism and nurture, and with the parents of infant candidates.

Baptism and Confirmation

- Holy Baptism.
- Emergency Baptism – not any less holy!
- Holy Baptism and Confirmation.
- Baptism and Confirmation in a vigil context (designed for evening services on the Eve of the Baptism of Christ, or on Saturdays in Epiphany or Eastertide, or on the Eve of All Saints' Day, or on Saturdays between All Saints' and Advent Sunday).
- Seasonal and Supplementary texts.

Rites of Affirmation: Appropriating Baptism

- Celebration after an initiation service outside the parish (for example, to welcome a baby baptized elsewhere, or to welcome those confirmed at the cathedral).
- Thanksgiving for Holy Baptism.
- Admission of the Baptized to Communion (that is, before confirmation).
- Affirmation of Baptismal Faith.
- Reception into the Communion of the Church of England.

Reconciliation and Restoration: Recovering Baptism

- Corporate service of Penitence.
- Reconciliation of a Penitent (that is, forms of service suitable for individual 'sacramental' confession).
- A Celebration of Wholeness and Healing.

The centrality of baptism

The model underlying this is of a journey through one's Christian life. The journey's beginning is officially marked by baptism, but there is acknowledgement that God is active in someone's life before that point.

After baptism, the rest of the journey consciously looks back to that starting point. The further stages (confirmation, affirmation of baptismal faith, reconciliation), while significant in their own right, are all ways of 'unpacking' or taking further the call and pattern established in baptism itself.

FAQ – How can we make the Baptism Service shorter and simpler?

The first thing to ask is, 'Is this the right question?' Often the key is how long the service *feels*, rather than how long the liturgical text is. It may be that plenty of movement, generous use of symbolism and action, wise choice of hymns and songs (maybe cutting some verses) and careful discipline about the sermon might go a long way to helping.

Then, make sure that you aren't including things that don't need to be in the service – note that there doesn't need to be a confession or a creed (other than the baptismal profession of faith).

There are also key parts of the printed service which are optional:

- The section in the Introduction beginning, 'Our Lord Jesus Christ has told us . . . '.
- The post-baptismal Commission for those able to answer for themselves (beginning, 'Those who are baptized are called to worship . . . ').
- The post-baptismal Commission for infants, *provided* that it is paraphrased or the contents covered in the sermon.
- The intercessions.

In addition,

- It is all right to have only one reading (the Gospel).
- Alternative (shorter) versions of The Decision (see *Common Worship: Christian Initiation*, p. 168) and the Profession of Faith (p. 178) can be used 'where there are strong pastoral reasons'.

See also below, 'Holy Baptism – structure and options', p. 70.

Key aspects of the Baptism Service

Proxy speaking

Note that parents and godparents speak 'for the candidate' at the Decision. They are not asked to state their own faith or commitment to Christ, though they are asked at the beginning of the service about their willingness to play their part in the child's incorporation into the Christian community.

Signing with the cross

The default position for this is at the Decision. The notes and rubrics suggest that sponsors, parents and godparents be invited to sign the candidates after the minister has done so.

Alternatively, it can come after the baptism, and, if so, it accompanies the prayer 'May God, who has received you by baptism . . . ' (see the guidance in Note 11, *CI*, p. 100).

Prayer over the water

Seasonal and responsive forms are given on p. 177 and in the Seasonal Provisions, starting on p. 150 of *CI*.

Quick Tip: Seasonal prayers over the water can be used at any time

Although many of the prayers over the water are in seasonal sections, the note on p. 150 of *CI* makes it clear that they can be used at any time, not just in their allocated season.

The mode of baptism

Dipping is the normative mode (with pouring a secondary option). The notes encourage 'the use of a substantial amount of water' (Note 12, *CI*, p. 100).

Threefold administration of water (once for each person of the Trinity) is commended as being of ancient tradition and reflective of Trinitarian faith, but it is not required.

Clothing after baptism

This is usually a practical necessity where the baptism is by submersion or immersion (whether of adults or children), and an optional text is provided which links this practical action with scriptural imagery. You don't need to use the words if no one is being clothed.

Prayers of intercession

Intercessions can be omitted in a Baptism Service, but their default *inclusion* (along with the suggestion in the rubric that those newly baptized or confirmed should take part in leading them) is intended to symbolize that taking part in the praying life of the Church for the world is an important element of Christian growth.

The giving of a candle

If individual candles are given, they can be lit from the 'large candle' (usually the Easter candle) which may be lit before the questions at the Decision. There is then a link between the candidates turning from darkness to the light of Christ (at the Decision) and taking their place as 'lights of the world' among the people of God (at the Sending Out).

FAQ – Why is the candle given at the <u>end</u> of the Baptism Service?

The giving of a lighted candle (which is optional) is seen as a symbol of mission, and so its default position is as part of the Sending Out at the very end of the service between the blessing and the dismissal.

It can, alternatively, take place immediately following the baptism itself, though the symbolism is not as strong at that point. There is also the added problem of what to do with the candle if it is given halfway through a service: blowing out the light of Christ does not feel like good symbolism.

At a service where baptism is accompanied by Confirmation, Affirmation and/or Reception, *all* candidates may be given candles.

Quick Tip: Use of oil in initiation

The use of oil in initiation is suggested in two places, but it is not compulsory in either. If you choose to use oil, you need to understand the difference between two different sorts:

- The Oil of Baptism (sometimes referred to as the Oil of Exorcism, Oil of Catechumens, or Oil of Initiation) is normally simple olive oil. It can be used for the Signing with the Cross immediately after the Decision.
- The Oil of Chrism is olive oil mixed with fragrant spices. It can be used for anointing immediately after baptism (accompanying the prayer for the Holy Spirit) or at Confirmation or Affirmation of Baptismal Faith. If there are candidates at a Confirmation service who are also being baptized, the chrism oil is used at their confirmation, not immediately following their baptism – Note 6, *CI*, p. 129.

For more general information on the use of oil, see *CI*, Note 10 on p. 100 and the commentary on pp. 343 and 345–8. The note says that it is 'appropriate' for the oil to have been consecrated by the bishop. This commonly happens on Maundy Thursday (or at some other time) in a service (sometimes known as a Chrism Eucharist) in which the oils for initiation and oil for healing are blessed by the bishop. In *Common Worship: Times and Season* there is a historical note which explains more about the oils (*TS*, p. 278) and material for receiving them into the local church on Maundy Thursday (*TS*, p. 292).

Holy Baptism – structure and options

Sections in *italic* are optional. An asterisk (*) indicates a choice of texts.

Preparation	
The Greeting	
Thanksgiving Prayer for a Child	An optional prayer (*CI*, p. 166) which focuses on the child's place in his or her human family, rather than the family of the Church.

Introduction*	The printed text 'or other words'.
The Collect*	Normally this would be the collect of the day or one appropriate to the season, but a more general collect for a baptism is provided in the text of the service itself (for example, *CI*, p. 64).
The Liturgy of the Word	
One or more readings from the Bible	On Sundays and Principal Feasts, Holy Days and Festivals these would normally be the lectionary readings of the day. Readings appropriate to baptism are provided on p. 167, and seasonal sets in the seasonal material on pp. 150–65. If only one reading is used, it is assumed that it is the Gospel.
Sermon	
The Liturgy of Baptism	
Informal presentation of candidate(s)	No fixed text. May include testimony.
Questions to candidate, congregation, parents and godparents	This (and the previous section) may come earlier, after the Introduction.
The Decision*	Alternative threefold set of questions (*CI*, p. 168) can be used if there are 'strong pastoral reasons'.
Signing with the cross	Oil may be used. Parents and godparents may join in. [May be delayed until immediately after baptism.]
Prayer over the water*	Lots of options, including responsive forms.
The Profession of Faith*	The default is the Apostles' Creed (in question-and-answer form). An alternative responsive form (*CI*, p. 178) can be used if there are 'strong pastoral reasons'.

The Baptism	
Clothing with a white robe	Optional words to accompany this are provided (for example, *CI*, p. 71).
Post-baptismal prayer ('May God, who has received you by baptism . . . ')	May be accompanied by anointing with chrism oil. [If the signing with the cross was not done earlier, it comes here, accompanying the post-baptismal prayer. The giving of a lighted candle may come after the prayer, if it is not being given at the end of the service.]
The Commission	May be paraphrased, or omitted if covered in the sermon.
The Prayers of Intercession*	Alternatively, these may come after the Welcome and Peace. Seasonal and alternative forms are provided (pp. 150–65 and 179) but are not compulsory.
Welcome and Peace	
The Sending Out	
The Blessing	
The Giving of a Lighted Candle	Either here or earlier, immediately following the post-baptismal prayer.
The Dismissal	

Quick Tip: The Thanksgiving Prayer for a Child

The structure above includes a Thanksgiving Prayer for a Child. This is not to be confused with the Thanksgiving for the Gift of a Child, which is a full service in its own right. If the latter has been used, the former is less appropriate in the Baptism Service.

FAQ – What is a 'strong pastoral reason'?

At the Decision and the Profession of Faith, alternative (shorter!) texts are provided for use where there are 'strong pastoral reasons'. This is clearly intended to discourage the use of these options as the norm, but a 'strong pastoral reason' is not defined anywhere. In effect, it is left for the minister to decide.

FAQ – Who can be a godparent in a Baptism Service?

A godparent must be baptized and confirmed (though the requirement for confirmation can be waived by the minister in 'any case in which in his [sic] judgement need so requires'). There is no formal minimum age, but the requirement of confirmation, as well as the actual role required of a godparent, suggests that there is a practical minimum.

The norm is to have three godparents (two of the same gender as the child), but the Canons allow for an absolute minimum of two if necessary. There is no maximum number. Parents can be godparents to their own child, as long as there is at least one other godparent.

For more, see Canon B 23.

Other key material in the package

Thanksgiving for the Gift of a Child

See the section in Chapter 6, Pastoral Services, for more detail about this service.

Confirmation

Confirmation in these services is seen, not as the completion of initiation begun in baptism, but as a significant pastoral rite along the way, involving prayer for the strengthening of the Holy Spirit as the candidates reach a new stage in their faith. Baptism itself is seen as complete sacramental initiation.

Common Worship: Christian Initiation prints in full a service of Baptism and Confirmation within a Holy Communion service. This is the default starting point. In addition, brief notes give guidance for

- Confirmation within a Communion service, but without baptisms (*CI*, pp. 124–5); and
- Baptism and Confirmation without Holy Communion (*CI*, pp. 126–7).

Admission of the Baptized to Communion

This material has been provided to assist parishes who (with their bishop's agreement) have adopted a pattern of admitting children to Communion before confirmation. The material is not compulsory in the form in which it is provided, and the fact that a full 'first Communion' service is not provided is significant. There is no intention here of providing a 'mini pseudo-confirmation'. The admission of children to Communion is important, but it is baptism that admits to Communion theologically, and this service merely marks a point after children have had some preparation and are ready to take up what is theirs in baptism. It is therefore designed to be fairly low-key, presided over by the parish priest (Note 3, *CI*, p. 188, makes clear that it should *not* normally be a bishop), and in the context of normal Sunday worship.

Affirmation of Baptismal Faith

The service of Affirmation of Baptismal Faith is designed for particular individuals who are conscious of a fresh work of God in their lives, and who wish publicly to commit themselves afresh to God, but who have already been baptized and confirmed.

Quick Tip: Affirmation of Baptismal Faith is not the same as Renewal of Baptismal Vows

Affirmation of Baptismal Faith should not be confused with the congregational renewal of baptismal vows. There is a service designed for the latter, called 'A Form for the Corporate Renewal of Baptismal Vows'. This often takes place at Easter. See the main volume, pp. 149ff., or *CI*, pp. 193ff.

The Affirmation of Baptismal Faith can take place as part of a baptism or confirmation service, but it can also take place as part of a normal Sunday service in a parish or chaplaincy context. It does not necessarily require the presence of the bishop, and may be presided over by a priest.

Quick Tip: Using water in an Affirmation of Baptismal Faith

In the service of Affirmation of Baptismal Faith the candidates can opt to sign themselves with water from the font. If this 'signing' is pushed to the limit, it could involve the candidates immersing themselves in a baptism pool. This is a pastorally useful option to suggest to someone who wants to be 're-baptized' on the basis that their infant baptism didn't use enough water and took place before they could remember it. The key is to make it clear that this is an affirmation of a previous baptism, and not itself a baptism. See *Common Worship: Christian Initiation*, p. 350, part of the Commentary material.

Reception into the Communion of the Church of England

This service is designed to welcome those of other Christian Churches (who have been episcopally confirmed) into the communion of the Church of England. If used in a normal Sunday service it may be presided over by a priest – the bishop's presence is not required (unless the candidate concerned is a priest).

N.B. This service is *not* connected with the admission to Holy Communion of those not yet confirmed. There is other material in *Common Worship: Christian Initiation* for that purpose – see below.

Reconciliation of a Penitent

This is the first material for private confession (sometimes called sacramental confession) to have been provided in the Church of England, since the material in The Visitation of the Sick in the *Book of Common Prayer*. It is provided for a different context from that in the Prayer Book (that is, serious sickness is not a prerequisite!), and is therefore not an authorized alternative to the Prayer Book service, but a commended form of service for a situation not covered by the Prayer Book. This means that the forms of service in *Common Worship* are neither mandatory nor restrictive, and other forms or none may be used. Even in the form in which they are printed, they stress that the ministry may take place in many different ways, formal or informal.

There is good practical guidance and an explanation of the purposes for which the material might be used on p. 266–9. This is supplemented by the Notes, which follow. In particular, Note 1 (*CI*, p. 270) reproduces the section from the *Guidelines for the Professional Conduct of the Clergy* (London: Church House Publishing, 2003) about confidentiality, and the so-called 'seal of the confessional'. Anyone using this material would do well to consult this section first. There is further theological reflection in the Commentary section (*CI*, pp. 351–4).

There are two forms of service which share a common structure. Form One follows a more traditional pattern which will be familiar to those who are used to the individual ministry of reconciliation. Form Two is labelled as an Individual Renewal of the Baptismal Covenant after Sin, and it draws more deliberately on baptismal imagery, and it is suggested it may take place at the font (Note 3, *CI*, p. 271). It is not so suitable for regular use as Form One. Though the services do not include it in detail, the rubrics and Note 7 (*CI*, p. 271) raise the possibility of offering prayer with laying on of hands and/or anointing, which could take place before the pronouncement of absolution.

Planning an initiation service: which elements do I need?

A service which includes combinations of some or all of Baptism, Confirmation, Affirmation and Reception can get quite complicated to plan. It is not always easy to work out from the notes and rubrics which elements need to be included and which can be omitted. There are lots of pages hidden away within *CI* which give particular guidelines for different combinations of candidates.

The following table tries to bring this together. It assumes that there will be confirmations, and therefore the bishop is present to preside over the service. It follows the basic pattern for a service with Baptism and Confirmation given in *CI*, starting on p. 108.

Items in *italic* in the first column are optional. A dot in a column indicates that an element must be included if there are candidates of this sort. Brackets indicate that the item is optional or that it does not apply in all circumstances.

Elements to be included	if there are candidates for . . .			
	Baptism	Confirmation	Affirmation	Reception
Preparation				
The Liturgy of the Word				
The Liturgy of Initiation				
Informal presentation of candidate(s)	(•)	(•)	(•)	(•)
Questions to baptism candidates ('Do you wish to be baptized?') – omitted if all baptism candidates are infants	(•)			
Question to other candidates ('Have you been baptized . . . ?')		•	•	•
Question to all candidates ('Are you ready with your own mouth . . . ?')	•	•	•	•
Testimony	(•)	(•)	(•)	(•)
Question to congregation ('Faith is the gift of God . . . will you welcome these candidates . . . ?') – N.B. if there are no candidates for baptism, omit 'Faith is . . . whom he is calling,' and start at 'People of God . . . '[1]	•	•	•	•
Question to parents and godparents (if baptism candidates include infants)	(•)			
The Decision	•	•	•	•
Signing with the cross – *with optional use of oil* [May come immediately after baptism instead]	•			
'Do not be ashamed to confess the faith . . . '	•			

---

1 *CI* does not specify this, though it does make sense. The earlier edition, *Common Worship: Initiation Services*, included the Confirmation Service without baptism candidates and dealt with this section in this way. The same is true of the stand-alone Affirmation of Baptismal Faith service, *CI*, p. 200.

'May God who has given you the desire . . . give you strength to continue . . . ' (only if there are no candidates for baptism and so the previous two sections have not been used)		(•)	(•)	(•)
Prayer over the water *If there are no candidates for baptism, the bishop may use instead the prayer at the font in CI, p. 125*	•			
The Profession of Faith	•	•	•	•
Question to baptismal candidates ('Is this your faith?')	(•)			
The Baptism	•			
Post-baptismal prayer ('May God, who has received you by baptism . . . ') – *with optional use of chrism if confirmation does not follow immediately* *[Signing with the Cross may happen here if it has not happened following the Decision. Giving of a lighted candle may happen here for the newly baptized if it is not to come at the end of the service.]*	•			
Declaration for Affirmation (*CI*, p. 203)			•	
Declaration for Reception (*CI*, p. 217)				•
Candidates sign themselves with water or are sprinkled with water		(•)	(•)	(•)
Prayer for faithfulness (' . . . Keep us faithful to our baptism . . . ')		•	•	•
Confirmation (prayer over confirmation candidates and prayer and laying a hand on each candidate) – *with optional use of chrism*		•		
Affirmation (prayer over Affirmation candidates and prayer and laying a hand on each candidate) *CI*, p. 204 – *with optional use of chrism*			•	
Prayer of Reception (prayer over Reception candidates and prayer and handshake for each candidate) *CI*, p. 218				•

Corporate prayer for all candidates ('Defend, O Lord, these your servants . . . ')	•	•	•	•
The Commission	(•)	(•)	(•)	(•)
The Prayers of Intercession	(•)	(•)	(•)	(•)
The Welcome ('We welcome you into the fellowship of faith . . . ')	•			
The Peace	•	•	•	•
The Liturgy of the Eucharist				
The Sending Out				
The Blessing	•	•	•	•
The Giving of a lighted Candle *(If candles are given to the newly baptized earlier in the service, they are not given out to others at this point.)*	(•)	(•)	(•)	(•)
The Dismissal	•	•	•	•

CI also provides a form of service for Affirmation of Baptismal Faith when it takes place in a local church with the local minister presiding (starting on p. 197) and gives further guidance about how this can be integrated into services of Holy Communion, A Service of the Word, or Morning or Evening Prayer (*CI*, pp. 209–11).

A 'stand-alone' version of Reception into the Communion of the Church of England is also provided (*CI*, pp. 211–22), again with guidance about integrating it into other regular services (*CI*, pp. 223–4).

Quick Tip: Presentation to whom?

At the Presentation of the Candidates, the candidates are presented to the *congregation*, not to the bishop. This may influence practical matters such as where they stand and in which direction they face.

FAQ – What is the difference between a godparent and a sponsor?

Godparents are appointed when the candidate for baptism is a child. Godparents have traditionally had a dual role: one is spiritual (to help their godchildren to grow in faith, and particularly to encourage them to come to be confirmed in due course), the other is social (to help and support parents more generally in the upbringing of a child).

Sponsors are appointed when the candidate for baptism is an adult, and the dual role of godparent is not appropriate. Their spiritual role, however, is similar, though exercised in ways that are appropriate for an adult. As with the appointment of godparents, there should be two or three sponsors, and they should have been baptized and (normally) confirmed. (Don't forget that when an adult is being baptized, the bishop should be informed at least a week before the service. See Canon B 24.2.)

Sponsors may also be appointed, in addition to godparents, when a child is being baptized. In this case, they have the spiritual role of supporting the child's growth in faith, without the responsibility of the social role. So, for instance, sponsors might be found from within the church to supplement godparents chosen by the child's parents.

Sponsors may also be appointed for candidates for confirmation or Affirmation of Baptismal Faith. They may present the candidate in the service and their ongoing role is to support the candidate in the journey of faith. The sponsors do not have to be the same persons who were godparents at the candidate's baptism.

For the detail, see: Canon B 23; Note 6, *CI*, p. 99; and the Commentary in *CI*, especially p. 342.

Further reading for this chapter

The key reading is the commentary in the Christian Initiation volume itself: *Common Worship: Christian Initiation*, London: Church House Publishing, 2006, pp. 314–54.

Paul Bradshaw (ed.), *A Companion to Common Worship – Vol. 1*, London: SPCK, 2001, Chapter 7; and Paul Bradshaw (ed.), *A Companion to Common Worship – Vol. 2*, London: SPCK, 2006, Chapters 6 and 8.

Colin Buchanan, *Infant Baptism in Common Worship*, Grove Worship Series 163, Cambridge: Grove Books, 2001.

Mark Earey, Trevor Lloyd and Ian Tarrant (eds), *Connecting with Baptism: A Practical Guide to Christian Initiation Today*, London: Church House Publishing, 2007.

Mark Earey and Gilly Myers (eds), *Common Worship Today – Study Edition*, Nottingham: St John's Extension Studies, 2007, Chapter 8.

Trevor Lloyd, *Thanksgiving for the Gift of a Child*, Grove Worship Series 165, Cambridge: Grove Books, 2001.

Gilly Myers, *Using Common Worship: Initiation Services – A Practical Guide to the New Services*, London: Church House Publishing, 2000 – based on the 1998 version of the services, but *does* take account of the loosening up that came later.

Michael Perham, *New Handbook of Pastoral Liturgy*, London: SPCK, 2000, Chapters 22 and 23.

Phillip Tovey, David Kennedy and Andrew Atherstone, *Common Worship Reconciliation and Restoration: A Commentary*, Grove Worship Series 187, Cambridge: Grove Books, 2006.

6

Pastoral Services

The thinking behind the services

The *Common Worship* pastoral services all work on the following assumptions:

- That they are part of a larger whole – the journey of each individual from birth to death.
- That for each element (birth, marriage, healing, death) the Church should provide key public liturgical events and lots of 'private' pastoral resources which make connections with the public liturgy. Thus the provision caters for the whole process, not just the public moments. So, for instance, as well as material for the funeral, *Common Worship* also includes material that can be used with someone approaching the end of his or her life.

Where can I find pastoral services?

Common Worship: Pastoral Services is the obvious central place in which to find all the pastoral services, but some are also found in other parts of *Common Worship*.

- Thanksgiving for the Gift of a Child is in *Common Worship: Christian Initiation* and the *Common Worship* main volume.
- Emergency Baptism is also in *Common Worship: Christian Initiation*.
- A Celebration of Wholeness and Healing is also in *Common Worship: Christian Initiation*, in the Reconciliation section.
- The Service of Laying on of Hands with Prayer and Anointing at a Celebration of Holy Communion is also included in *Common Worship Times and Seasons: President's Edition for Holy Communion*, where some of the propers for Marriage and Funerals are also reproduced.

Quick Tip: Pastoral Introductions

The Marriage Service, Thanksgiving for the Gift of a Child, and the Funeral Service each have a Pastoral Introduction printed before the service itself (on pp. 102, 201 and 256, respectively). Each of these Introductions includes some brief explanation about the service and is intended to be read by the congregation before the service begins. In practice this will only be possible if it is printed in any locally produced order of service, or if it is reproduced in other material (for instance, a leaflet left after a funeral visit, or given to a marriage couple, or sent to parents enquiring about Baptism or Thanksgiving for their child).

What's in the Pastoral Services volume?

The key services are as follows:

- Wholeness and Healing material.
- Marriage and related material.
- Emergency Baptism.
- Thanksgiving for the Gift of a Child.
- Funeral and related material.

See below for more detail on some of these sections.

Quick Tip: Check which edition of the *Pastoral Services* volume you have

Common Worship: Pastoral Services first came out in 2000. A second edition came out in 2005, which has extra material: Psalms for Use at Funeral and Memorial Services; the Series One Marriage Service and Series One burial services. The Series One services are basically the revised services from the 1928 Prayer Book. Like *Common Worship*, they are now authorized 'until further resolution of the Synod'. Because of this extra material in the second edition, the page numbering of the two editions differs from p. 392 onwards.

The material below assumes the second edition – check your copy to see which version you have.

Wholeness and healing

Material is provided for use in three different contexts:

Diocese or deanery

A Celebration of Wholeness and Healing

- Intended for a 'large-scale' service.
- Not primarily envisaged as a eucharistic service (the 'sacramental high-point' is the anointing, laying on of hands and prayer for individuals).
- Not expected to be as frequent as the ministry of healing in a parish.
- Could be used for an annual service in celebration of the healing ministry (to which, for example, local health service staff could be invited).

This material could also work in a Team Ministry, local cluster, or with ecumenical partners in a locality, or in a conference or other large gathering context.

Parish

Laying on of Hands and Anointing

This is material for use at a regular 'healing service' in a parish or other local context (such as a hospital, school, college or prison chaplaincy).

A form of words is provided for the laying on of hands (*PS*, p. 21), but any suitable form can be used.

Figure 3 shows how an Order One Holy Communion service can be adapted using this material, to make a service with a strong element of healing and wholeness.

Individual

Ministry to the Sick

This is for use with those who are ill, either in their homes or in hospital. It includes orders for a full celebration of Holy Communion (Order One, and Order One traditional language) and orders for the distribution of communion from the reserved sacrament (Order One and Order Two).

Figure 3: A Healing Service with Holy Communion

Prayer for Individuals in Public Worship

This consists of two pages of guidance notes (*PS*, pp. 48–9) intended for churches which offer regular ministry to individuals either during or after ordinary Sunday services.

Figure 4 shows the points within an Order One Holy Communion service at which the guidance notes suggest prayer with individuals might be offered: as part of the intercessions; as an option during or after the distribution of Holy Communion; at the end of the service.

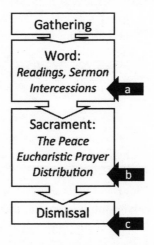

Figure 4: Possible positions for individual prayer

Prayers for Protection and Peace

This is provided for use by any minister in situations where 'it would be pastorally helpful to pray with those suffering from a sense of disturbance or unrest'. This is clearly distinguished from the ministry of exorcism, which may only be exercised by priests authorized by the bishop (see Notes 1, 2 and 3 on *PS*, p. 94).

Quick Tip: Other places to look for healing-related material

As well as the Wholeness and Healing section in the *Pastoral Services* volume, there are other places where this material can be found:

In *New Patterns for Worship* (p. 451) there is a sample outline Service of Healing which shows how to use other material.

In the main volume there is a Thanksgiving for the Healing Ministry of the Church (pp. 50–3) which includes the possibility of laying on of hands and anointing. This is designed to be used as part of Morning or Evening Prayer, rather than as a stand-alone service. See Note 8 on p. 58 of the main volume for details.

The Celebration of Wholeness and Healing service is also printed in *Common Worship: Christian Initiation*, starting on p. 290. Here it is placed alongside material for Reconciliation and Restoration, recognizing that wholeness is needed in every aspect of our being. For similar reasons, the guidance about Prayer for Individuals in Public Worship is also printed in the *Christian Initiation* volume (*CI*, pp. 264–5) and prayer with laying on of hands and/or anointing is suggested in the material for Reconciliation of a Penitent (Note 7, *CI*, p. 271).

Laying on of hands and anointing is also provided for in Ministry at the Time of Death in the Funerals section of the *Pastoral Services* volume (*PS*, p. 226).

If you are planning a Holy Communion service with prayer for healing, there are suitable proper prefaces (short and extended) in *PS*, pp. 36–8.

The form of service for a Celebration of Holy Communion at Home or in Hospital (Order One, *PS*, p. 53) includes Eucharistic Prayer E, with the extended preface for healing and wholeness, but other choices can be made.

Quick Tip: Readings for a healing service

If you are looking for readings for a service focusing on prayer for wholeness and healing, there is a useful table of suggestions on pp. 44–5 of *PS*.

Thinking theologically

Don't miss the Theological Introduction to the Wholeness and Healing section (*PS*, pp. 9–11), which puts prayer for individuals' needs in a bigger theological context. Some of this thinking has also been put more concisely in the form of Introductions which could be used by the minister either at the start of a service or near the time for prayers of intercession or for individuals (*PS*, pp. 42–3).

FAQ – Where do we get the oil for anointing from?

The oil may have been previously consecrated by the bishop at a diocesan service (for example, a Maundy Thursday Chrism Eucharist), or by the priest, using the form in the Celebration of Wholeness and Healing (*PS*, p. 20) or one of the alternative forms provided in the Supplementary Texts (*PS*, pp. 46f.) – see Note 2, *PS*, p. 40.

For more information about the Chrism Eucharist, and the place of the oils in it, see the Historical Note in *Common Worship: Times and Season* (*TS*, p. 278). There is also material for receiving consecrated oils into the local church on Maundy Thursday (*TS*, p. 292). If you are using oils consecrated at a Chrism Eucharist, make sure you use the right one – you will need, for these purposes, the oil of the sick, not the oil of baptism or the oil of chrism.

Quick Tip: Receiving prayer on behalf of someone else

The guidelines for Prayer for Individuals mention that prayer with laying on of hands may be received on behalf of someone else, who is not present (*PS*, p. 48, Note 2). In this case, be careful to establish whether the third party has given permission for (or requested) such prayer, or for information about their condition to be shared.

FAQ – Who can lay on hands and anoint?

Anyone who has been invited to do so by the person presiding at the service, and who has been appropriately prepared, may assist with the laying on of hands.

Anointing with oil is normally administered by a priest, but may be delegated to other ministers 'authorized for this ministry under Canon B 37' (*PS*, p. 40, Note 1). However, while Canon B 37 specifies that the oil must have been consecrated by a priest or by the bishop, it does not give specific restrictions about who is authorized to do the anointing itself. The canon simply assumes that the person laying on hands or anointing is the priest, because it was written at a time when there were no services or texts for this ministry, and the context is assumed to be a person who is ill at home and has called for the minister.

Marriage and related material

A range of material is provided. Some of the key points are as follows.

Prayers at the Calling of Banns

Two prayers are suggested in the Supplementary Texts (*PS*, p. 135), but any other suitable form may be used.

Marriage

The main options are:

- The Marriage Service.
- The Marriage Service within the Order for the Celebration of Holy Communion – Note 11 encourages 'communicant members of the Church' to see this as a possibility and, in any case, urges the couple to receive Communion soon after their marriage.
- Series One Marriage ('A Form of Solemnization of Matrimony') – *PS*, pp. 418ff.

Quick Tip: Ecumenical Marriage Service

There is a further option: The Marriage of Christians from Different Churches. This is a form of service produced by the Joint Liturgical Group. It is *not* printed in *Common Worship: Pastoral Services* (it is published separately, by Canterbury Press), but it *is* a legal form of service for Anglican marriage where the couple are from different Christian Churches. For more on this, and for other guidance when a minister of another Christian Church is to be involved in a Church of England Marriage Service, see Note 13 on p. 134 of *PS*.

FAQ – When are the couple legally married?

The emphasis in *Common Worship* is on recognizing the whole service as important, rather than focusing on a particular 'moment'. The service itself, however, in the Preface and in the Proclamation, singles out the giving of consent and the exchange of vows as the key acts which make the marriage.

The exchange of rings is normally important too, and neither the rubrics nor the notes explicitly make it optional (though the option for either one ring or two rings to be used is made clear). However, in the Preface and Proclamation the giving of rings is described as a 'token' or a 'declaration' of the primary acts of giving consent and exchanging vows.

The Registration of the marriage comes immediately after it is solemnized (see Note 10, *PS*, p. 134), but is itself a formal recording of what has taken place, rather than an integral part of the marriage.

Quick Tip: Giving away the bride?

Note that the 'giving away' of the bride is optional, and that words for this are not provided in the main text but in the Notes (Note 6, *PS*, p. 133). The phrasing is careful: 'Who brings *[not "gives"]* this woman to be married to this man?'. It is made clear that if there is to be a giving away, it does not have to be the bride's father who does it.

Alternatively, earlier in the service, both sets of parents may be asked to entrust the bride and groom to one another (Note 6).

Prayer and Dedication after a Civil Marriage

This is a revised form of the service which has existed for many years. It has been brought into line with the *Common Worship* marriage material.

Thanksgiving for Marriage

An outline Order of Service is provided, designed to cover the following situations:

- Renewal of marriage vows, when a number of couples reaffirm their vows together.
- Celebration of a wedding anniversary, for a particular couple or couples.
- Following a time of separation or difficulty, for a particular couple.

The service may be adapted for home or church use and may be combined with Holy Communion. A worked out example of its use for the Renewal of Vows is also provided (*PS*, pp. 186ff.).

Quick Tip: A 'traditional' service

If a couple ask for a 'traditional' service, it is worth checking whether they want the 1662 Prayer Book service, or the Series One version (in the second edition of *Common Worship: Pastoral Services*) which is basically 'Prayer Book, as revised in 1928', or the *Common Worship* Marriage Service, but with traditional language vows (*PS*, p. 151).

The structure of the Marriage Service

Like every *Common Worship* service, the Marriage Service begins with a page setting out the basic structure of the service (*PS*, p. 103). However, this is laid out as basically two main sections: Introduction and The Marriage. To get a feel for the flow of the service, the structure page for the Marriage Service within a Celebration of Holy Communion (*PS*, p. 115) is much clearer. Here it is possible to see the 'eucharistic' shape which is actually there in the *Common Worship* Marriage Service whether there is Holy Communion or not. If you lay out the basic Marriage Service structure (without Communion) in the same way, you get this:

The Gathering

The Welcome.
Preface.
The Declarations.
The Collect.

The Liturgy of the Word

Readings.
Sermon.

The Marriage

The Vows.
The Giving of Rings.
The Proclamation.
The Blessing of the Marriage.
Registration of the Marriage.
Prayers.

The Dismissal

Marriage – some key choices

The table below brings together some of the main options and choices which are mentioned in the rubrics and Notes. This might be useful to help the minister in service planning, in discussion with the couple.

The Gathering	The couple may arrive together, rather than the bride arriving separately.
	If the bride arrives on her own, she does not have to be accompanied by anyone, and if she is it does not have to be her father.
The Welcome	The three texts provided in this section are all optional and can be omitted or replaced (note the rubrics).
Preface	Note the brackets in the line: ' . . . in which children are [born and] nurtured', which allows for some sensitivity if there are already children from this (or a previous) relationship.
	An alternative version (closer to the form in the *ASB*) is provided on p. 136 of *PS*.
The Declarations	The *Book of Common Prayer* version may be used as an alternative (*PS*, p. 133, Note 7).
[Entrusting by Parents]	If this is used, it comes after the couple have made their declarations and before the congregation are asked to pledge their support. It is not, therefore, a straight swap for the traditional 'giving away'. For a suggested form of words, see *PS*, p. 133, Note 6.
The Collect	
The Liturgy of the Word	This whole section, or just the sermon, may instead come after the blessing of the marriage (*PS*, p. 132, Note 5).
Readings	A selection of suggestions is provided on pp. 137–49 of *PS*, but these are not the only possibilities.
	At least one Bible reading must be used (see the rubric, *PS*, p. 107).
Sermon	

The Marriage	
[The 'Giving Away']	This is optional, and does not need to be done by the bride's father. A form of words is provided (*PS*, p. 133, Note 6) which asks, 'Who brings this woman . . . ?' It is not used if the Entrusting by Parents has been used earlier.
The Vows	An alternative contemporary language form (in which the bride promises to obey) is provided on p. 150 of *PS*. A second alternative, in traditional language with 'obey', is provided on p. 151 of *PS*, with the option to omit 'obey' if preferred.
The Giving of Rings	An alternative Prayer at the Giving of the Rings is provided on p. 151 of *PS*. A text is provided if only one ring is given. The Notes offer an alternative pattern where the rings are exchanged first and then the bride and groom say the words together (*PS*, p. 133, Note 8).
The Proclamation	
The Blessing of the Marriage	A series of alternative forms is provided (*PS*, pp. 152–5). [If the marriage takes place in a service of Holy Communion, the Blessing of the Marriage can follow the Lord's Prayer.]
[Readings and Sermon]	This is the alternative position of the sermon, or the readings and sermon, if they are not used earlier. If readings and sermon do come here, it probably helps the flow of the service if the Registration is moved to its alternative position at the very end.

Registration of the Marriage	The Registration takes place at this point, or at the end of the service (*PS*, p. 134, Note 10).*
Prayers	A huge selection of prayers of various sorts is provided on pp. 156–68. Note 9 (p. 133) encourages the involvement of the couple in choosing or writing the prayers. The Prayers conclude with the Lord's Prayer, and it is worth asking the couple which version they would prefer.
The Dismissal	
[Registration of the Marriage]	This is the alternative position for the Registration, if it has not taken place earlier.

FAQ – Do we have to say the vows line by line?

Common Worship assumes that the bride and groom will each repeat their vows after the minister, but also mentions that they could read them instead (presumably from a suitably large-print card or order of service held by the minister). The couple could, of course, choose to learn the words by heart.

There is also specific allowance for the bride to answer first in the Declarations section and to make her vow first, rather than following the groom each time. See *PS*, p. 133, Note 7.

---

* The Note actually says the Registration comes 'after the Proclamation', even though it is printed after the Blessing of the Marriage, but this seems to be to anchor the Registration, given that the Blessing of the Marriage can be moved to a later position if the service includes Holy Communion.

Thanksgiving for the Gift of a Child

Who is it for?

The notes (*PS*, p. 200) suggest three possible scenarios for which this service is designed:

Parents seeking a baptism soon

The Thanksgiving can act as a preliminary to baptism, held in advance, perhaps seen as part of the preparation for baptism. It has the advantage of needing no 'preparation' and can therefore be organized more speedily than a baptism.

Parents who want to allow for adult baptism later

Parents who plan to 'let their children make their own decision when they are old enough'. This would include parents in a Church of England congregation who have roots in a Baptist tradition (or other church practising only believers' baptism), who may be looking for some sort of 'dedication' service. The Thanksgiving can form the basis of such a service, perhaps with the addition of some questions to the parents about their intention to bring the child up within the Church.

Parents who do not want a baptism

Parents who are looking for some way of saying 'Thank you' for their child, but feel that the level of commitment to the Church and the Christian faith assumed in the Baptism Service is not right for them at the moment.

The Thanksgiving can be usefully offered to such parents as an alternative to baptism, or as a first step to exploring their own faith, which may or may not lead to baptism for their child, sooner or later.

Quick Tip: The clue is in the title

The title of the service – Thanksgiving for the *Gift* (rather than 'Birth') of a Child – makes it clear that it can be used for adopted children, and also makes it easier to use for an older child, not just a recently born baby.

What form can the service take?

Again, the notes suggest three possibilities which are spelt out below:

- **Private** – The service can be made as low-key as required, even to be used in the family home with just a few family and friends present. Alternatively it could be used with one child as a 'stand-alone' private service in church.
- **Public** – A 'stand-alone' service for several children in church – perhaps once a month on a Sunday afternoon.
- **Public, within regular worship** – The Thanksgiving (or parts thereof) can be incorporated into a main Sunday service.

The basic structure of the service

Introduction

Reading(s) and Sermon

- One Bible reading is required (though there could be more), and there is a list of suggestions on p. 207 of *PS*.
- The sermon may be omitted 'if occasion requires'.

Thanksgiving and Blessing

- [A 'supporting friend' may present the child].
- Questions to parents.
- Prayer of thanks.
- Asking for name.
- Prayer of Blessing for the child.
- Prayer for parents.

Giving of the Gospel

- A Gospel is presented.
- [Question to 'supporting friends'].
- [Question to wider family and friends].

Prayers

- Including Lord's Prayer.

Ending

- Blessing of the congregation.

Quick Tip: Who can bless the child?

Though the service includes a blessing of the child, the prayer has been carefully phrased to allow for the service to be led in its entirety by a Reader or other lay minister.

What are 'supporting friends'?

In a Thanksgiving service, the parents have the option to appoint 'supporting friends', who may be asked questions about their support of child and parents. If a baptism is to follow, these may or may not be the same people as the godparents at the baptism.

FAQ – Who can be a Supporting Friend in a Thanksgiving service?

Anyone whom the parents ask to take on that role – typically, they would be a small group of family and friends of the parents. There are no restrictions about who may be asked – they do not have to be baptized or confirmed, and there is no limit as to how many may be chosen, or what gender they are.

What do Supporting Friends do?

There are three points within the service at which they may take an active role:

- Standing with the parents at the point of thanksgiving, and presenting the child or children to the minister.
- Giving the name of the child to the minister before the blessing of the child.
- Pledging their support for child and parent/s, 'with God's help', after the giving of the Gospel.

There is also an optional question to the congregation about their support of the family and child.

Quick Tip: A Thanksgiving Register and Certificate

The notes stress the importance of there being a register of Thanksgiving services and of giving a certificate that makes it clear that the service was not a baptism.

Funerals and related material

Common Worship: Pastoral Services contains a range of material, to provide not only for the funeral itself but also for the pastoral opportunities that precede and follow the funeral service.

Ministry at the Time of Death

This section includes resources to use with someone who is dying, including prayer with laying on of hands and anointing, reception of Communion, and the ministry of reconciliation.

There are also resources for 'Prayer when someone has just died' (*PS*, pp. 234ff.), which might be used at the bedside of someone who has died, with the family gathered around, but could also be adapted for personal use when hearing of a death by phone (for instance), or when announcing the recent death of a congregation member in a Sunday service.

Quick Tip: Familiar texts

Note 3 stresses the importance of using texts familiar to the dying person.

Before the Funeral

Includes:

* 'At home before the funeral', which could be used when hearing of someone's death, or as part of a visit to a family.

- 'For those unable to be present at the funeral' is based on the Funeral Service itself and is ideal to use with someone who is unable to be at the funeral (perhaps because of distance, or because they are themselves in hospital or housebound).
- 'Receiving the Coffin at Church before the Funeral' may be used 'at the beginning of the Funeral Service, or earlier in the day, or on the day before the Funeral' (opening Note).

Quick Tip: Texts to accompany the placing of symbols

The optional texts to accompany the placing of 'suitable symbols of the life and faith of the departed person' are found in this section, and also in the supplementary texts ('Some Texts which may be used by the Minister' – starting on p. 295 of *PS*).

FAQ – Can we include non-biblical readings in the funeral?

It's common for families of the deceased to ask for poems or other readings to be included in the service. There is nothing to prevent these being included in principle (though the minister has responsibility for determining their suitability). However, any such readings should *supplement* and not replace the Bible reading(s) (see Note 2 to the Funeral Service, *PS*, p. 291).

The Funeral itself

The key options are:

- **The Outline Order for Funerals.** This is not the same as the structure outline of The Funeral Service (for which, see *PS*, p. 258). Rather, it is an authorized order of service in its own right. This provides a very flexible structure (like A Service of the Word) with authorized words required only at the prayers of Commendation and Committal (and at the confession, if there is one).

Quick Tip: Using the Outline Order for maximum flexibility

The Outline Order for Funerals is the key to getting maximum flexibility in a *Common Worship* funeral service. It is the obvious starting point for a funeral at the crematorium chapel, where time is likely to be tight.

- **The Funeral Service.** This is the 'default' worked-out order for a funeral.
- **The Funeral Service within a Celebration of Holy Communion** is not quite a full order of service, but a series of suitable resources drawing on Funeral and Holy Communion material. See below for more detail.
- **The Outline Order for the Funeral of a Child.** An outline form is given, with lots of resources, to allow for maximum pastoral flexibility.
- **The Series One Burial Service** ('An Order for the Burial of the Dead' – *PS*, pp. 430ff.).

Quick Tip: 'He was no angel . . . ' – when feelings are mixed

Not everyone feels sad at a funeral or thankful for the life that has ended. There are several things within the *Common Worship* resources which may helpfully be used or adapted in these situations:

- The inclusion of Prayers of Penitence, with space for some silence, may be an opportunity for some recognition of difficult times, but this needs to be handled carefully to avoid the impression that it's the living who bear the blame.
- The prayers of intercession included in The Funeral Service (*PS*, p. 265) include a line, 'Heal the memories of hurt and failure'.
- In the Resources section, Prayer 26 (*PS*, p. 354) expands the thought with the line, ' . . . we also remember times when it was hard for us to understand, to forgive and to be forgiven. Heal our memories of hurt and failure . . . '

There are also a number of other prayers for circumstances which may be particularly difficult (for example, After a Short Life, After a Violent Death, After a Suicide, etc.) on pp. 358–61 of *PS*.

A funeral including Holy Communion

If the funeral takes place within a service of Holy Communion, the Liturgy of the Sacrament (beginning at the Peace and going through until the Prayer after Communion) fits in after the Prayers and before the Commendation and Farewell.

In that case:

- A Gospel reading becomes compulsory (optional 'Alleluia' acclamations are provided).
- Words to introduce the Peace are provided.
- A prayer at the preparation of the table is provided.
- Two short proper prefaces are provided, and one extended preface (for use with Eucharistic Prayers A, B or E) with optional congregational responses.
- Prayer after Communion includes the option to use the prayer, 'Heavenly Father, in your Son Jesus Christ you have given us a true faith . . . ' as a congregational Post Communion prayer.

FAQ – What book will they have at the crematorium?

The book of funeral services often found at crematoria (containing Church of England, Roman Catholic and Free Church forms, and a selection of hymns) is produced by an ecumenical organization called the Churches' Group on Funeral Services at Cemeteries and Crematoria.

The most recent editions (2001 and 2009) contain a basic form of the *Common Worship* funeral service and the Series One form. Some crematoria may also have copies of the *Common Worship* Funeral Service in booklet form (a purple booklet, with fuller provision than the Crematoria book).

Quick Tip: The sermon and a tribute

The Notes make a clear distinction between any tribute (which will be about the person who has died) and the sermon (which is 'to proclaim the gospel in the context of the death of this particular person'). The Funeral Service and the Outline Order for Funerals both indicate that the norm is for the tribute to come in the early part of the service and not to be confused with the sermon, which comes after the readings. It is acknowledged, however, that 'if occasion demands' the tribute can be 'woven into the sermon'. The key seems to be making sure that the Gospel does not get overshadowed by a lengthy or powerful tribute. See *PS*, p. 291, Notes 4 and 5.

After the funeral

'At home after the funeral' can be used immediately following the funeral or several days later.

Quick Tip: Burial in a mausoleum

There is a committal text for burial in a vault, mausoleum or brick grave on p. 292 of *PS*, at the end of Note 8.

The Burial of Ashes

Two options are provided at the prayer of committal. One is the traditional prayer (' . . . ashes to ashes, dust to dust . . . '), and the other draws on the imagery of the potter and the clay (*PS*, p. 328). This second form allows the 'ashes to ashes, dust to dust' text to be used at the crematorium, and not repeated at the burial of ashes. Similarly, there are two options for a committal at the crematorium, depending on whether the primary committal is seen as the cremation or the later burial of cremated remains. The table below shows two ways of combining these options.

	At the cremation (*PS*, p. 269)	At the burial of ashes (*PS*, p. 328)
If the burial of ashes is seen as the primary committal	' . . . and now, in preparation for burial, we give *his/her* body to be cremated. We look for the fullness of the resurrection, when Christ shall gather all his saints to reign with him in glory for ever.'	' . . . we now commit *his/her* mortal remains to the ground: earth to earth, ashes to ashes, dust to dust: in sure and certain hope of the resurrection to eternal life . . . '
If the cremation is seen as the primary committal	' . . . and now we commit *his/her* body to be cremated: earth to earth, ashes to ashes, dust to dust: in sure and certain hope of the resurrection to eternal life . . . '	'God our Father, in loving care your hand has created us, and as the potter fashions the clay you have formed us in your image . . . We claim your love today, as we return these ashes to the ground in sure and certain hope of the resurrection to eternal life.'

Memorial Service

This is designed for use several weeks after the funeral itself. If the service is to take place on the day of the funeral (after a private committal at the crematorium, for instance) or very soon after, then the Funeral Service itself should be used (without the Committal) rather than this service (*PS*, p. 334, Note 2).

There is an outline form of service (and an outline which includes Communion). A worked-out version is provided as a sample.

Quick Tip: The Memorial Service and annual memorials

The Memorial Service in *Common Worship: Pastoral Services* is *not* intended for corporate memorial or thanksgiving services which many churches offer around All Souls' day or at other times of the year, to which the bereaved are invited. There is material which may be adapted for this purpose in *Common Worship: Times and Seasons* (in the Eucharist of the Commemoration of the Faithful Departed, *TS*, pp. 562ff.).

Alternative (non-eucharistic) provision was available in *The Promise of His Glory*, pp. 74–82 (see Note 3, *PS*, p. 3, which refers to this material). *The Promise of His Glory* (London: Church House Publishing/Mowbray, 1991) was a volume of seasonal resources, commended by the House of Bishops, for the period from All Saints to Candlemas. It is now out of print (but sometimes available second-hand). Much of it has found its way (in revised form) into *Common Worship: Times and Seasons*, but this is one example of material that has been lost.

Resources

- Prayers for Use with the Dying and at Funeral and Memorial Services – a vast array of material for different stages of the journey.
- Bible Readings and Psalms for Use at Funeral and Memorial Services – texts printed out in full, and a useful table of 'further readings' which lists other possibilities, with a brief sentence summary of the passage (useful for preparing a funeral sermon).
- Canticles for Use at Funeral and Memorial Services.

Quick Tip: Blessing a grave

If you ever need to bless a grave, there's a prayer on p. 296 of *PS*.

Using the *Common Worship* funeral material

The table that follows gives some ideas about how to use the range of
material in actual practice.

The funeral of . . .	The use of *Common Worship* material . . .
Joan, aged 71, died of pneumonia leaving husband, two sons and four grandchildren. Neither she nor any of her family had any connection with the Church. The family wanted a simple service at the crematorium.	• The Outline Order for Funerals was used as the basis for the service. • At a follow-up visit a Pastoral Assistant left Joan's widower a card which included a couple of prayers used at the funeral and the first parts of the Pastoral Introduction (*PS*, p. 256).
Japhet, aged 55, a churchwarden of St Peter's, who died suddenly of a heart attack leaving his wife and three grown-up children.	• The news of Japhet's death was announced at church the following Sunday and material from 'Prayer when someone has just died' was used (*PS*, p. 234). • His body was received into church the night before the funeral and a vigil was kept until midnight (using 'Receiving the Coffin at Church before the Funeral' and 'A Funeral Vigil' – *PS*, pp. 242–52). • The coffin was covered with a pall (a white cloth) as a sign of baptism accompanied by words from *PS*, p. 295. • The funeral service in church included Holy Communion and concluded with the committal. The crematorium was a long way from the church, and so the coffin was taken there by the funeral director, accompanied by one of

	Japhet's family, but there was no further ceremony when they got there.
	• His ashes were interred in the churchyard a week later, with just close family present, and using the second form of committal on p. 328 of *PS*.
Agnes, a widow aged 88, who died peacefully at home. She had been a regular at All Saints' Church since she was a girl, and when she became too frail to attend the 8 a.m. service, she had Communion at home. Her sister Eileen, aged 93, was in a nursing home nearby, and too frail to come to the funeral.	• Agnes's coffin was received into church the evening before the funeral without ceremony, except that her old Bible was placed on the coffin accompanied by words from *PS*, p. 296. • The funeral was a simple affair in church, followed by a burial in the local cemetery. • Two members of the congregation went to be with Eileen at the time of the service, and used material from 'For those Unable to be Present at the Funeral' (*PS*, pp. 240–1).
Susan, aged 45, a local councillor, who died after a long and very public battle with cancer.	• The funeral service was held in church followed by a cremation. • Two weeks later a Memorial Service was held in the church, attended by many local people.
Stefan, a five-year-old member of the congregation of St Jude's, who was killed in a road accident.	• The vicar used material from 'On the morning of the Funeral' with the family before they set off for the service. • The service was in church, using material from 'Resources for the Funeral of a Child'.
Brian, aged 65, a regular member of St Philip's, who died of cancer.	• Material from 'Ministry at the Time of Death' was used with Brian in the hospice before and at his death.

He left a widow, Di, three children and five grandchildren.	• Material from 'At Home before the Funeral' was used in pastoral visits after his death and before the funeral. • The crematorium was some distance away, and so the cremation was held in the morning with just close family present, and was followed by an afternoon service in church using material from 'The Funeral Service' and 'A Memorial Service'. • On returning to the house, a Pastoral Assistant used the prayer, 'Open, O God the door of this house' from 'At Home After the Funeral' (*PS*, p. 318) with Di.

Further reading for this chapter

General

Paul Bradshaw (ed.), *A Companion to Common Worship – Vol. 2*, London: SPCK, 2006, Chapters 7, 9 and 10.

Mark Earey and Gilly Myers (eds), *Common Worship Today – Study Edition*, Nottingham: St John's Extension Studies, 2007, Chapter 12.

Michael Perham, *New Handbook of Pastoral Liturgy*, London: SPCK, 2000, Chapters 24, 25, 26 and 28.

Wholeness and healing

Colin Buchanan, *Services for Wholeness and Healing: The Common Worship Orders*, Grove Worship Series 161, Cambridge: Grove Books, 2000.

Carolyn Headley, *Home Communion: A Practical Guide*, Grove Worship Series 157, Cambridge: Grove Books, 2000; and *The Laying on of Hands and Anointing*, Grove Worship Series 172, Cambridge: Grove Books, 2002.

A Time to Heal: A Report by the House of Bishops on the Healing Ministry, London: Church House Publishing, 2000.

Marriage

Andrew Body, *Making the Most of Weddings*, London: Church House Publishing, 2007.

Stephen Lake, *Using Common Worship: Marriage – A Practical Guide to the New Services*, London: Church House Publishing, 2000.

Stephen Lake, *Welcoming Marriage: A Practical and Pastoral Guide to the New Legislation*, London: Church House Publishing, 2009.

Peter Moger (compiler), *Church of England Marriage Services with Selected Hymns, Readings and Prayers*, London: Church House Publishing, 2010.

Charles Read and Anna de Lange, *Common Worship Marriage*, Grove Worship Series 162, Cambridge: Grove Books, 2001.

Thanksgiving for the Gift of a Child

Mark Earey, Trevor Lloyd and Ian Tarrant (eds), *Connecting with Baptism: A Practical Guide to Christian Initiation Today*, London: Church House Publishing, 2007, Chapter D2, pp. 126–31.

Trevor Lloyd, *Thanksgiving for the Gift of a Child: A Commentary on the Common Worship Service*, Grove Worship Series 165, Cambridge: Grove Books, 2001.

Funerals

Anne Horton, *Using Common Worship: Funerals – A Practical Guide to the New Services*, London: Church Home Publishing, 2000.

Trevor Lloyd, *Dying and Death Step by Step: A Funerals Flowchart*, Grove Worship Series 160, Cambridge: Grove Books, 2000.

7

Daily Prayer

What do we have to use?

Patterns of weekday daily prayer (sometimes known as the Daily Office) are covered by the requirements of A Service of the Word. This means that *Common Worship: Daily Prayer* is not the only authorized alternative to the services of Morning and Evening Prayer in the *Book of Common Prayer*. Rather, the *Common Worship* services are simply one possible outworking of A Service of the Word for daily prayer. Any other forms which also fulfil the requirements of A Service of the Word are equally acceptable. See the table in Chapter 3, pp. 49–50, to see what those requirements are.

Quick Tip: Which bits of the service are necessary?

In Morning and Evening Prayer in *Common Worship: Daily Prayer* certain elements are marked as necessary (with a line down the left-hand margin) and all else is described as optional. However, the necessary parts are only 'necessary' in order to 'maintain the integrity' of the service in the minds of those who put the services together. Because the services are covered by A Service of the Word, none of it is 'compulsory', in the absolute sense, in the form in which it is printed. See *DP*, p. 103, Note 1, for the detail.

Where to find daily prayer services

- The obvious place to find daily worship resources is in *Common Worship: Daily Prayer*.
- The *Common Worship* services of Prayer During the Day and Night Prayer (along with selected psalms) can also be found in *Time to Pray* (London: Church House Publishing, 2006).

- Night Prayer is also available in the *Common Worship* main volume. The contemporary language version (starting on p. 81) is the same as the service in *Common Worship: Daily Prayer*. The traditional language version (starting on p. 89) is only printed in the main volume.
- If you want to use the Prayer Book version of Morning and Evening Prayer for weekday worship, you will find those in the *Common Worship* main volume, starting on p. 59.

Quick Tip: Watch out for the Preliminary Edition

Like some other parts of *Common Worship*, the Daily Prayer volume was originally published in a different form from the current version. The first version was produced in paperback, clearly marked 'Preliminary Edition' on the spine. The idea was to get a lot of feedback from experimental use, which could then feed into an improved final version. This means that the preliminary edition works perfectly well on its own, but if you have copies and try to use them alongside the final version, you'll come unstuck, as significant changes were made.

FAQ – Do clergy have to use *Common Worship: Daily Prayer* every day?

The Canons of the Church of England expect every ordained minister to 'be diligent in daily prayer' and in particular to say Morning and Evening Prayer every day, either alone or with others (Canon C 26). Because A Service of the Word is the authorized alternative to Morning and Evening Prayer in *The Book of Common Prayer*, anything which fulfils the requirements of a Service of the Word would be appropriate for clergy to use, including, but not restricted to, the forms of service in *Common Worship: Daily Prayer*.

> **Quick Tip: Don't try to use the main volume for daily prayer**
>
> The *Common Worship* forms of Morning and Evening Prayer in the main volume (starting on page 29) are designed for use on *Sundays*, and are not very suitable for daily prayer use.

What's in *Common Worship: Daily Prayer*?

There are three main types of service in *Common Worship: Daily Prayer*:

Prayer During the Day	A different form for each day of the week during Ordinary Time.
	A different form for each season for Seasonal Time.
Morning and Evening Prayer	A different form for each day of the week during Ordinary Time.
	A different form for each season for Seasonal Time.
Night Prayer	One form, provided with variations of psalm, short reading and collect for each day of the week during Ordinary Time.
	One form, provided with variations of psalm, short reading, collect and blessing for each day of the week during Seasonal Time.

The book also contains a wealth of other resource material to support daily prayer, including canticles, prayers, forms of intercession and the *Common Worship* version of the psalms, with a psalm prayer for each (see below, Chapter 8, for more information on the *Common Worship* Psalter).

Quick Tip: Good companions for *Common Worship: Daily Prayer*

For travelling, or other situations when the full book is too heavy or bulky, an alternative is to use *Celebrating Daily Prayer* (London: Continuum, 2005). This uses *Common Worship* texts (the Psalter, Canticles, prayers) but in a more compressed format drawn from *Celebrating Common Prayer* (London: Mowbray, 1992), a book which inspired many aspects of *Common Worship: Daily Prayer*.

  Reflections for Daily Prayer (Church House Publishing, published annually) are daily Bible reading notes which follow the *Common Worship* weekday lectionary. See Chapter 2 for information on the weekday lectionary.

Prayer During the Day – what is it for?

Prayer During the Day is designed as a short and simple 'one-a-day' service, which can be used in different ways:

- Instead of Morning or Evening Prayer – a good 'way in' for someone beginning to explore patterns of regular daily prayer, for whom Morning and Evening Prayer might be too 'heavy' or complicated.
- In addition to Morning and Evening Prayer (as a midday office).
- With Night Prayer as a simple 'two-a-day' pattern of daily prayer.

Planning guide for Morning and Evening Prayer

Quick Tip: Daily Prayer on the web

On the Church of England website you can get Morning and Evening Prayer for today and tomorrow, with the appropriate psalms, readings and collect, in both *Common Worship* and *Book of Common Prayer* forms. You can use it on-screen, or cut and paste to your word processor.

Decisions for every service

- Find the **reading(s)** (from the *Common Worship* weekday lectionary – see above, p. 36). See below for more detail on choosing the psalm or psalms.
- Decide which pattern to use for the readings:
  either Psalm → OT reading → Canticle → NT reading
  or Psalm → Canticle → OT reading → NT reading
- Choose any **hymns** or music and decide where to put them in the service.
- Decide about the **Preparation** section – how will you use the options printed, and will you make use of any other options? For instance, the Acclamation of Christ at the Dawning of the Day (*DP*, pp. 108f.) can replace the Preparation at Morning Prayer, and the Blessing of Light (*DP*, pp. 110f.) can replace the Preparation at Evening Prayer. In addition, the forms of Penitence (*DP*, pp. 91–7) can replace the Preparation or be incorporated within it, at any service.
- Decide about **canticles** (scripture canticle; gospel canticle) – will you use the ones printed in the order, or one of the other options?
- Decide **how to say Psalms and canticles** – responsorially, antiphonally, together, with or without a pause, etc.
- Decide about the **Prayers and Conclusion** – will you use it as printed in the order, or will you use one of the Thanksgivings (*DP*, pp. 304–14) or the Prayers for Unity (*DP*, pp. 315f.) or Prayers at the Foot of the Cross (*DP*, pp. 317f.)?
- Decide about the **Collect** prayer – will you use the one printed in the order or the Collect of the Day (that is, set for that week)?
- Decide about the **Lord's Prayer** – which form will you use? Note the introductions to the different versions.
- Is it a **saint's day** or other special commemoration? What choices will that influence (readings, collect, etc.)?

Some choices are influenced by the time of year:

Ordinary Time	*Seasonal Time*
• Find the appropriate form of service. A different service is provided for each day of the week.	• Find the appropriate form of service. A different service is provided for each season.

- Choose the **psalm**(s) – the basic cycle is sequential, working through the Psalter psalm by psalm at Morning and Evening Prayer.

  If more than one psalm is set, will you use all of them, or just one (the one in bold)?

- Decide about **intercessions** – will you use the cycle of topics (pp. 362–3) or one of the fuller forms (pp. 366–76 and p. 396) or some other pattern?

- Choose the **psalm**(s) – in Seasonal Time the lectionary gives two possible sequences.

  The *first* is basically seasonal (that is a selection of psalms relating to the season);

  the *second* is essentially sequential (like the psalms in Ordinary Time)

- Decide about **intercessions** – will you use the seasonal cycle of topics (pp. 364–5) or one of the fuller seasonal forms (pp. 377–95) or some other pattern?

There are some really helpful notes and guidance in *Common Worship: Daily Prayer* itself (pp. ix–xx and 100–7).

Quick Tip: Finding the text of the Lord's Prayer

The Lord's Prayer is not printed out each time in the actual services in *Common Worship: Daily Prayer*, but it is printed in both modern and traditional forms inside the front or back cover.

Other useful resources

There are four other useful resources tucked away in the 'Additional Material for Morning and Evening Prayer'.

Prayer for the Unity of the Church (*DP*, pp. 315f.)
A very simple service which might make a useful framework for a short service or regular acts of prayer in the Week of Prayer for Christian Unity, as well as at other times.

Prayers at the Foot of the Cross (*DP*, pp. 317f.)
Particularly commended as a form of prayer on Fridays (though not in

seasons of celebration), with a focus on a cross and suggestions for symbolic actions and prayers.

A Commemoration of the Resurrection (*DP*, pp. 319–24)
A short service designed for early on a Sunday morning, especially in the Easter season.

Vigil Office (*DP*, pp. 325–30)
A special pattern for Evening Prayer, for use on the evening before a Sunday or Principal Feast.

Further reading for this chapter

Paul Bradshaw (ed.), *A Companion to Common Worship – Vol. 2*, London: SPCK, 2006, Chapter 1.

Christopher Cocksworth and Jeremy Fletcher, *Common Worship Daily Prayer*, Grove Worship Series 166, Cambridge: Grove Books, 2001.

Mark Earey and Gilly Myers (eds), *Common Worship Today – Study Edition*, Nottingham: St John's Extension Studies, 2007, Chapter 11.

Jeremy Fletcher and Gilly Myers, *Using Common Worship: Daily Prayer*, London: Church House Publishing, 2002.

Michael Perham, *New Handbook of Pastoral Liturgy*, London: SPCK, 2000, Chapter 20.

8

The *Common Worship* Psalter

What is a 'Psalter'?

'Psalter' is just another word for a book containing the psalms, especially if designed for use in worship. The *Common Worship* Psalter means the psalms in their *Common Worship* version.

A Service of the Word specifies a psalm, or a hymn or song based on a psalm or on another scriptural passage, as one of the elements 'normally' required in a service, whether a main service on a Sunday, or a form of daily prayer (see main volume, p. 27, Note 6).

Where to find the *Common Worship* Psalter

The *Common Worship* version of the psalms can be found in the following places:

- The *Common Worship* main volume.
- *Common Worship: Daily Prayer*, where each psalm is given a suggested refrain, and a psalm prayer (sometimes called a psalm collect).
- A selection of psalms for use in funerals can be found in *Common Worship: Pastoral Services* (pp. 392–405).

Where does the *Common Worship* Psalter come from?

The *Common Worship* version of the psalms is based on the version in the 1979 *Book of Common Prayer* of the Episcopal Church of the USA, checked against the original languages and then put alongside the Prayer Book Psalter, so that there are deliberate echoes of the 'Coverdale' psalms, which those who are used to Prayer Book Evensong may recognize.

> ### Quick Tip: Psalms pointed for chanting
>
> If you are looking for pointed versions of the *Common Worship* psalms (that is, with marks to show where to change note when chanting the psalms), you need the resource *Music for Common Worship IV: The Common Worship Psalter* in which the psalms and canticles are pointed for use with Anglican Chant. This is published by the Royal School of Church Music (www.rscm.com).

What do I need to know?

- Where to find the alternative doxology.
- What the 'diamond' is for.
- What to do with the optional refrains.
- What to do with the optional psalm prayers.
- What the *CW* Psalter does with the so-called 'cursing psalms'.

The alternative doxology

A doxology ('Glory to the Father, and to the Son . . . ' – sometimes called the *Gloria Patri*) is traditionally added to the end of a psalm when it is recited in the context of Morning or Evening Prayer. The doxology also gives each psalm a Christian context for interpretation.

In *Common Worship: Daily Prayer* there is an alternative version of the doxology ('Glory to God, Source of all being, Eternal Word and Holy Spirit . . . ') – *DP*, p. 648.

The 'diamond'

The diamond in the middle of each verse marks a point at which those using the psalm may choose to pause (a common tradition in monastic communities). This breaks each verse into two sections and some psalms work well with each verse split between two groups (one group takes the first half of the verse; the other takes the second half, that is, after the diamond). For example, Psalm 142 would work well with this pattern.

The optional refrains

In *Common Worship: Daily Prayer* each psalm is printed with an optional refrain (sometimes called an 'antiphon'). This can be used in different ways:

- At the beginning and end of the psalm (after the doxology, if this is included).
- At the beginning and end and at several points during the psalm (marked in *Common Worship: Daily Prayer* with a special marker [R]). This can be a useful means of congregational participation if the psalm itself is being said or sung by a single voice.

The optional Psalm Prayers

In *Common Worship: Daily Prayer* each psalm is given a Christian prayer to conclude it. There are different ways of using these psalm prayers. The prayer can be said by the congregation together or by the leader. The big question is: in what order?

- The psalm prayers can be used *instead* of the doxology, as they fulfil a similar purpose.
- If the doxology is to be used as well (not recommended), the psalm prayer comes *afterwards*.
- If you are using the doxology, the refrain and the psalm prayer (definitely not recommended) they come in that order.

The key point is to leave a suitable silence before using the psalm prayer to 'collect together' the individual reflections and prayers of those present.

The 'cursing psalms'

Some psalms, or parts of psalms, are sometimes avoided in worship, because they are seen as inappropriate to put into the mouths of Christian worshippers today. In some versions of the Psalter, these psalms are placed in brackets, to show that they can be omitted. The *Common Worship* Psalter does not use brackets to suggest the omission of any parts of the psalms.

FAQ – Do we have to use the *Common Worship* Psalter?

Any translation of the psalms may be used in Church of England churches, not just the one published in the *Common Worship* books.

Quick Tip: Two spellings for 'blessed'

You may notice that in the psalms in *Common Worship* you sometimes come across 'blessed' spelled as 'blest'. The idea is to help with pronunciation: 'blessed' is pronounced as two syllables ('bless-ed'); 'blest' is pronounced as one syllable. See *DP*, p. 648, Note 1.

Further reading for this chapter

Paul Bradshaw (ed.), *A Companion to Common Worship – Vol. 1*, London: SPCK, 2001, Chapter 10.

Mark Earey and Gilly Myers (eds), *Common Worship Today – Study Edition*, Nottingham: St John's Extension Studies, 2007, Chapter 16.

9

Miscellaneous

Who can do what?

Generally speaking, *Common Worship* distinguishes clearly between what must be done or said by a priest (or bishop) and what can be done or said by a deacon or lay person.

- In a Holy Communion service, if the rubric says 'The **president** says . . . ' it means either a priest or a bishop.
- If the rubric does not specify, or says 'A **minister** says . . . ', then the scope is broader, and could include a deacon, Reader or other person involved in leading the service.

Another key place to look for guidance is the long note on 'Ministries' in the General Notes in the main volume on pp. 158–9.

The Note on 'Ministries'

The note on Ministries is hidden away in the main volume, undiscovered by many. However, it contains useful guidance about the appropriate liturgical roles of priests and deacons in services of Holy Communion. It is important to recognize that much of it is *only* guidance (note the use of phrases like 'In some traditions . . . '), but it is guidance that is hard to find in other places. The key points are outlined below. See the *Common Worship* main volume, pp. 158–9, for the full, official version.

The liturgical ministry of all

Members of the congregation might share in the leadership of the service in the following ways:

- doing Bible readings;

- leading prayers of intercession;
- assisting with the distribution of Holy Communion (if authorized to do so by the bishop).

The liturgical ministry of a deacon

The note suggests this might include:

- bringing in the Book of the Gospels;
- leading the invitation to confession;
- reading the Gospel;
- preaching;
- leading or taking a part in the prayers of intercession;
- the preparation of the table;
- sharing in the distribution of Communion;
- the ablutions (that is, washing the Communion cup and plate);
- the dismissal.

In some churches the deacon also gives the invitation at The Peace ('Let us offer one another a sign of peace') and leads the introduction to the memorial acclamations in the Eucharistic Prayer ('Great is the mystery of faith . . . ' and equivalents). Neither of these, however, is mentioned specifically in the Note on Ministries, though in the Holy Communion services, Note 18 (main volume, p. 333) mentions that the deacon might lead the congregational acclamations in Eucharistic Prayer F.

The note on Ministries specifically mentions that the deacon's role can make a useful model for any leadership which complements that of the president, giving a pattern that can be adapted for assisting priests, Readers or other authorized lay ministers.

The liturgical ministry of the president

This would normally include:

- saying the opening Greeting;
- giving the Absolution;
- saying the Collect;
- introducing the Peace;
- leading the Eucharistic Prayer;
- giving the Blessing.

The note goes on to recognize that there are occasions when parts of this list (but not the Eucharistic Prayer) can or must be delegated to a deacon, Reader or authorized lay minister. For instance, this might be a helpful way of using the leadership gifts of a Reader in a parish in which worship is almost always eucharistic. In other contexts it might be necessary (rather than just helpful): for instance, in a multi-parish benefice where the priest is presiding at several services and may only arrive part-way through. Though this is not ideal practice, it is good to see it recognized as part of the reality in some contexts.

The Lord's Prayer

The Lord's Prayer occurs in most *Common Worship* services, and where it is printed in full it is usually printed in both a contemporary and traditional language version. Often, each has a different 'cue line' to help congregations to know which version to join in with.

These two forms, with the cue lines used in Holy Communion Order One, are as follows:

Common Worship **contemporary language version**	*Common Worship* **traditional language version** *Also known as the 'modified traditional version'.*
As our Saviour taught us, so we pray	Let us pray with confidence as our Saviour has taught us
Our Father in heaven, **hallowed be your name,** **your kingdom come,** **your will be done,** **on earth as in heaven.** **Give us today our daily bread.** **Forgive us our sins** **as we forgive those who sin** ** against us.** **Lead us not into temptation** **but deliver us from evil.** **For the kingdom, the power,** **and the glory are yours,** **now and for ever.** **Amen.**	**Our Father, who art in heaven,** **hallowed be thy name;** **thy kingdom come;** **thy will be done;** **on earth as it is in heaven.** **Give us this day our daily bread.** **And forgive us our trespasses,** **as we forgive those who trespass** ** against us.** **And lead us not into temptation;** **but deliver us from evil.** **For thine is the kingdom,** **the power and the glory,** **for ever and ever.** **Amen.**

There are two other versions which may be used with *Common Worship* services:

Ecumenical contemporary language version	The *Book of Common Prayer* version
Produced by the English Language Liturgical Consultation (ELLC) and printed in the main volume on p. 106 for use 'on suitable occasions'. What these occasions might be are not spelt out, but they might include ecumenical services. It is, for instance, the modern language version printed in The Methodist Worship Book 1999.	*Sometimes referred to as 'the traditional version', this form may be used in any* Common Worship *service, instead of the versions printed above (see Rule 6 on p. 525 of the main volume).* *It is also the form of the Lord's Prayer used in Holy Communion Order Two in traditional language.*

As we look for the coming of the kingdom, so we pray
 	
Our Father in heaven,
hallowed be your name,
your kingdom come,
your will be done,
on earth as in heaven.
Give us today our daily bread.
Forgive us our sins
as we forgive those who sin
   against us.
Save us from the time of trial
and deliver us from evil.
For the kingdom, the power,
and the glory are yours,
now and for ever.
Amen.
	Our Father, which art in heaven,
	hallowed be thy name;
	thy kingdom come;
	thy will be done,
	in earth as it is in heaven.
	Give us this day our daily bread.
	And forgive us our trespasses,
	as we forgive them that trespass
	   against us.
	And lead us not into temptation;
	but deliver us from evil.
	For thine is the kingdom,
	the power and the glory,
	for ever and ever.
	Amen.

Visual Liturgy

What is it?

Visual Liturgy is service planning software based on *Common Worship*.

What version do I need?

There have been several versions of *Visual Liturgy*. The latest is *Visual Liturgy Live* for *Common Worship*. The basic details are:

- It costs £125 (or £52 upgrade from *VL* 4).
- Annual subscriptions (after the first year) cost £52 per annum and provide you with updates, new texts and so on. If you choose not to subscribe, the existing software will continue to work.
- It requires the Windows operating system (there is no Mac version).
- Team licences are available (these allow you to install the software on any number of computers in a 'team' (which might be one parish or chaplaincy) – for example, ministers, administrators, worship leaders, etc.).

For more information see the website – www.visualliturgylive.net.

What can you do with it?

- Get **liturgical texts** – all the *Common Worship* material is included, and subscribers get updates with any new material.
- Choose hymns and songs:
  - some full texts are included;
  - you can get some tunes as midi files;
  - you can browse by first line to get texts;
  - you can also use it to help with choices – search by theme, Bible passage, etc.
- Get the **Collect prayer and readings** for a given occasion – perhaps for printing on a notice sheet?
- Plan services and produce service sheets:
  - choosing liturgical items and hymns;
  - producing leader's text, congregation text, etc.;
  - produce OHP slides.
- Plan service **rotas**:
  - allocate tasks across a parish or team of churches.
- Produce **lectionary** reports, which give you lists of Bible readings for use in rotas, etc.

Do I need it?

- Depends how you like to plan worship.
- Depends how you produce printed orders of service.

Music for *Common Worship*

There are music settings (traditional tunes) for some of the eucharistic prayers in the *President's Edition*, the Festivals volume, *Common Worship Times and Seasons: President's Edition for Holy Communion* and *Common Worship: Holy Week and Easter.* This last volume also includes some chants for the services of Holy Week and the Easter Liturgy (for instance, the Proclamation of the Cross and the Exsultet).

In addition, the Royal School of Church Music (RSCM) has produced several volumes of music resources designed specifically to be used with *Common Worship.*

- *Music for Common Worship I: Music for Sunday Services.*
- *Music for Common Worship II: Music for the President.*
- *Music for Common Worship III: A Basic Guide.*
- *Music for Common Worship IV: The Common Worship Psalter – Psalms and Canticles Pointed for Use with Anglican Chant* (words only).
- *Music for Common Worship V: The Common Worship Psalter with Chants.*
- *Music for Common Worship VI: Night Prayer* (modern language).
- *Music for Common Worship VII: Compline* (in traditional language – published in association with the Plainsong and Medieval Music Society).

These are all available direct from the RSCM (see their online shop at www.rscm.com).

There are several resources to help with choosing hymns, songs and other music to go with the *Common Worship* lectionary (or the ecumenical version). For instance:

- *Sing God's Glory: Hymns for Sundays and Holy Days, Years A, B & C*, Norwich: Canterbury Press, latest edition 2007.
- *Sunday by Sunday* (RSCM) – this quarterly publication for RSCM members gives ideas for hymns, songs, anthems, organ music, etc.

for each Sunday of the *Common Worship* Principal Service Lectionary.

* *Sunday by Sunday: Music for the Second Service Lectionary* (RSCM/Norwich: Canterbury Press, 2008) gives suggestions for all three years of the *Common Worship* Second Service Lectionary (often used for evening services).

Visual Liturgy Live also gives lectionary-based hymn and song suggestions, as do many hymn books in their full music editions. Lots of websites also give this sort of guidance, though many originate in North America and will be based on the *Revised Common Lectionary*, rather than the *Common Worship* version.

Further reading for this chapter

Who can do what?

Michael Perham, *New Handbook of Pastoral Liturgy*, London: SPCK, 2000, Chapters 3 and 4.

Glossary

Here's the bluffer's guide to sounding like an expert on *Common Worship*. The list includes some key terms that you need in order to understand *Common Worship*, plus a number of other more general liturgical terms.

Where do these jargon terms come from?

Jargon develops in different ways:

- Sometimes it happens when the name for something in an ancient language (whose meaning was obvious at the time) continues to be used even when the language is not generally used. This is the case with many of the Latin names for prayers and objects (such as 'Magnificat' below).
- Sometimes it happens when one group of people use a term whose meaning is clear in itself, but it is being used in a technical, rather than generic, sense (such as 'Prayer Book' below). This makes it possible for the hearer to misunderstand.
- Sometimes it is simply a shorthand way of saying something that would otherwise sound laboured if repeated in full each time.

Note: In the definitions below, an asterisked term (*) indicates that the word appears as a separate glossary entry.

Ablutions   The cleaning of the chalice* and paten* after Holy
                Communion. May also refer to the eating and drinking of
                consecrated bread and wine that is left over.

Acclamation   A brief act of spoken or sung praise, such as the Alleluia
                Acclamation which may precede the Gospel reading, or
                the Memorial Acclamation which may occur during the

Eucharistic Prayer (such as 'Christ has died, Christ is risen, Christ will come again').

Acolyte — A person who carries a candle in a procession in church.

Agnus Dei — A song which begins 'Lamb of God', often said or sung in Communion services. From the first line of the Latin version.

Alb — Long, white garment with narrow sleeves, worn over the top of a black cassock by clergy. A 'cassock-alb' is similar, but is designed so that you don't need to wear a separate cassock underneath.

Altar — The table at which the Eucharist* is celebrated. The term is used in some Church of England churches, but in *Common Worship* the term 'Holy Table' is used.

Altar call — The opportunity to respond to the gospel message, usually by coming to the front of church either during, or at the end of, a service.

Ambo — See 'Lectern'.

Anamnesis — The part of a Eucharistic Prayer when we explicitly 'remember' Jesus, as he told the apostles to do at the Last Supper. The term comes from the Greek for 'remembrance'.

Anthem — A piece sung by the choir alone.

Aumbry — A place to put consecrated bread and wine from Holy Communion, which is to be used later. Some churches may also use it to store consecrated oil for anointing in baptism or healing.

Benedictus — a) The Song of Zechariah from Luke 1.68–79, which begins 'Blessed be the Lord, the God of Israel'. The title is taken from the first line of the Latin version.
b) The short acclamation 'Blessed is he who comes in the name of the Lord' which often follows the Sanctus* in the Eucharistic Prayer. Sometimes called the *Benedictus qui venit* (from the first line of the Latin version), to distinguish it from (a) above.

Burse	A cover for a folded corporal.* A burse is square, made of two pieces of board joined on one side, and usually decorated with material in the liturgical colour of the season. When the corporal is taken out of it, it is sometimes placed standing on the Holy Table. Often comes in a set with a matching veil.*
Canticle	Literally, 'a song'. In liturgical terms can be either a song derived from a Bible passage or from other Christian writings.
Chalice	The cup which holds the wine for Holy Communion, especially if it is made out of silver or other precious metal.
Chasuble	Vestment shaped like a poncho, worn in some churches by a priest (especially the president at the Eucharist) over the top of an alb* and stole.*
Chrism	Oil mixed with fragrant spices, as a sign of the Holy Spirit and the messianic age. May be used to anoint the newly baptized, accompanying the prayer after baptism. It can also be used at Confirmation or Affirmation of Baptismal Faith.
Ciborium	A container for holding Communion wafers. Usually looks like a chalice* with a lid. The term can also be used, on an architectural scale, to describe a free-standing canopy which stands over the altar.*
Collect	A particular form of prayer which is designed to 'collect together' the prayers which have preceded it (which may have been silent or spoken). In *Common Worship* there is a collect provided for each Sunday and Feast Day, as well as collect-style prayers for other occasions. The word 'collect' is usually pronounced with the emphasis on the *first* syllable. The collect prayer has nothing to do with the collection of money.
Compline	Another name for Night Prayer, the last of the daily services, designed to be said before retiring to bed.
Corporal	A square white cloth laid on the altar.* The chalice* and paten* for Communion are placed on it.

Glossary

Crucifer	A person who carries the processional cross in a procession in church.
Deacon	In the Anglican, Orthodox and Roman Catholic Churches, an ordained person who is not also a priest or bishop. Has a different meaning in the Baptist Church and some other Free Churches.
Doxology	An ascription of praise added to the end of prayers (such as, 'the kingdom, the power and the glory are yours', at the end of the Lord's Prayer). From the Greek, meaning 'glory-words'.
Epiclesis	A Greek word meaning 'calling down'. Refers to part of the Eucharistic Prayer which 'calls down' the Holy Spirit (or God generally) on the bread and wine and/or the congregation.
Eucharist	Another name for Holy Communion. From the Greek word for 'thanksgiving'.
Eucharistic Prayer	The prayer of thanksgiving over the bread and wine at Holy Communion. Sometimes it is referred to as the prayer of consecration, or the *anaphora* or the *canon*.
Fall	Technical term for a coloured or decorated cloth which hangs down ('falls') from a lectern* or pulpit.
Frontal	Technical term for a large decorated or coloured cloth that hangs down the front of an altar.*
Gradual	Historically a chant, but often today refers to a hymn, sung before the Gospel reading.
Introit	An opening psalm or hymn, usually sung by a choir on its own. From the Latin word for 'Entrance'.
Lavabo	The ceremonial washing of the priest's hands before the eucharistic prayer* is said.
Lectern	A tall stand to hold a book, at which the Bible reading may take place. Sometimes called an 'ambo'.
Lectionary	List of Bible readings assigned to particular Sundays, festivals or weekdays. Sometimes refers to a book in which these readings are printed out in full.

Litany	A long, responsive form of prayer (see *CW* main volume, p. 111).
Magnificat	Mary's song from Luke 1.46–55, which begins 'My soul magnifies . . . ' The title is taken from the first line of the Latin version.
Narrative of Institution	Also known as 'Institution Narrative' – the part of a Eucharistic Prayer* which gives the account of Jesus at the Last Supper.
Nunc Dimittis	Simeon's song from Luke 2.29–32, which begins 'Now you dismiss your servant . . . ' The title is taken from the first line of the Latin version.
Offertory	Sometimes this term is used to mean the collection of money in a service. It is sometimes used in a more technical sense to refer to the point in the service where the bread and wine for Holy Communion are brought to the holy table. Sometimes the two happen at more or less the same time. An 'offertory procession' usually means people bringing bread and wine to the holy table up the aisle from the back of the church. An 'offertory hymn' is the hymn sung at this point in the service, while the collection is taken and/or the bread and wine are brought forward.
Office	Usually means a form of service which is not a Eucharist. Daily Prayer services are often referred to as the Daily Office, and Pastoral Services are sometimes called Occasional Offices.
Pall	a) A small, square piece of card, covered in white linen. It is placed on top of a chalice,* especially when the chalice has wine in it. b) A white cloth which can be placed over a coffin at a funeral as a sign of baptism (echoing the white robe traditionally put on by the newly baptized, which lives on in the English tradition of christening gowns).
Paten	The plate which holds the bread for Communion, especially if it is made out of silver or other precious metal.

Glossary

Pointing	A way of marking the Psalms (or Canticles*) for chanting, showing where the note changes.
Prayer Book	Can refer to any service book. Often a reference to the Church of England's *Book of Common Prayer* of 1662.
Preface	Literally the 'proclamation' (from Latin). It means the first part of the Eucharistic Prayer* (up to the 'Holy, holy . . . '), which is praise rather than petition. A 'proper preface' is therefore praise which is 'proper' (that is, appropriate) to this day or season. It is also used in the *Common Worship* Marriage Service as a title for the long introduction at the beginning of the service, which begins, 'In the presence of God . . . ' (see *Common Worship: Pastoral Services*, p. 105).
Presbyter	Another word for a priest. From the Greek word for 'elder'.
President	The leader presiding over (overseeing) the whole act of worship. At Holy Communion this would be a priest or bishop, and certain parts of the service (such as the Eucharistic Prayer)* can be led only by this person.
Proper	In liturgy generally, 'propers' are texts which are 'appropriate' to a particular season, feast, saint's day or theme. Classically the term applies to Proper Prefaces* (the part of a Eucharistic Prayer* which can be varied according to the season or day) but the term can also apply to other variable texts such as introductions to confession, blessings or post communion prayers. In *Common Worship* the term is also used to refer to sets of Bible readings which the lectionary* appoints for given dates in Ordinary Time (see above, Chapter 2).
Psalter	Another name for the book of Psalms. Often means a book in which the Psalms are set out or 'pointed'* for chanting.
Purificator	The white cloth used to wipe the rim of the chalice* after someone has drunk from it.
Pyx	A small container for consecrated Communion wafers, often used when taking Communion to the sick.

Robes	A general term for special clothes worn during worship by clergy and others such as servers,* acolytes,* crucifers,* choir members, etc. See also 'Vestments'.
Rubrics	The instructions in a service (such as 'The president uses these or other suitable words' or 'This response is used') as opposed to the words which are spoken or sung. From the Latin, meaning 'red words' because traditionally (and in *Common Worship*) these instructions were printed in red rather than black.
Sacristan	Person responsible for making practical arrangements for Holy Communion services, such as ensuring there are supplies of bread and wine and so on.
Sanctuary	Usually refers to the area of a church building around the main holy table, especially if this is separated from the rest of the church by rails of some sort.
Sanctus	The song which begins 'Holy, holy, holy', often said or sung during the Eucharistic Prayer* in Communion services. From the first line of the Latin version.
Server	Someone who assists during the service, and especially at Holy Communion.
Stole	Long scarf-like vestment worn over the top of a surplice* or alb*. Worn hanging straight down by a priest and over the left shoulder and across the chest by a deacon.*
Surplice	Flowing white robe with wide sleeves worn over the top of a black cassock.
Sursum corda	The opening dialogue part of the Eucharistic Prayer: 'Lift up your hearts' (from the Latin).
Tabernacle	Literally means 'tent' or 'dwelling'. A place in which consecrated bread and wine are kept for the purposes of taking Communion to the sick and/or to be used as a focus for prayer and devotion. Also sometimes called an aumbry.*
Thurible	An incense burner which is held suspended on chains so that the incense can be 'waved' in the direction of people or objects as a sign of setting them apart for worship.

Glossary

Veil
A square cloth, usually in the liturgical colour of the season, sometimes used to cover the chalice* and paten* on the holy table. Often comes in a set with a matching burse.*

Vestments
Special clothes worn by clergy, especially at the Eucharist.*

Vestry
The room in which clergy (and perhaps others, such as servers* or choir members) put on their robes to lead worship.

List of QTs and FAQs

3 Services of the Word

4 Holy Communion

7 Daily Prayer

8 The Common Worship Psalter

Index

Page numbers in *italic* type indicate that the related entry is found in a table or box on that page.

Glossary items are not included in this index, so you might want to look there as well.

Index

Ash Wednesday *27*, *30*, 41
ashes, burial of 102, *103*, *106*
Athanasian Creed 57
authorized services 2, 3, 5, 14, *14*, *15–16*, *18*, *44*, 47, 76, *83*, 99, 109, *110*

banns of marriage 88
baptism 5, 7, 10, 12, 65–73, *75*, 76, *77–9*, *80*, *83*, 95
  as admission to communion 74
  believer's 95
  centrality of 67
  complete sacramental initiation 73
  Emergency 66, 82, 83
  immersion 69
  in relation to Thanksgiving for a Child 95
  liturgical colour 22
  making the service shorter *67*
  mode of 68
  of adults *80*
  structure and options *70–2*
  Thanksgiving for Baptism 66
  use of oil *70*
Baptism of Christ 66
Bible 11, 30, *32*, *see also* scripture
  placed on coffin *106*
  versions allowed *35*
Bible reading notes 37, *112*
Bible readings 30, *53*, 120
  at a funeral *99*, 104
  at a healing service *87*
  at a marriage 91, *92–3*
  at A Service of the Word *49*
  at baptism services *67*, *71*
  at Thanksgiving for Child 96
  Common of the Saints 29
  daily prayer 113
  finding via *Visual Liturgy* 124
  how many must we have? *35*
  in Night Prayer *111*
  related to collects 44, *45*
Bible Sunday *25*
biblical references, index 12
bishop 3, 12, *14*, *15*, 42, 63, *70*, 74, *75*, *75*, 76, *78*, *79*, *80*, 86, *87*, *88*, *104*, 120, 121

black book, *see* main volume
Blessed Virgin Mary 22
Blessing a grave *104*
Blessing of Light 113
blessing
  of a child 96, *97*
  of a Marriage 91, *93*
  of non-communicants *61*
blessings 8, 10, *16*, 29, *50*, *69*, *111*, 121
Book of Common Prayer 1–2, *15*, *44*, 47, *58*, 110, *110*
calendar 24
Collect for Second Sunday of Advent *25*
collects *44*, *45*
collects derived from *41*, *43*
collects in Morning and Evening Prayer 40
communion service 52
Lord's Prayer *123*
marriage declarations *92*
marriage service *90*
material in CW main volume 5
Morning and Evening Prayer 5, 109, *112*
ordinal 9
psalms *35*, 116
Visitation of the Sick 75
booklets, for CW services 12
Breaking of the Bread *53*
burial *106*
burial of ashes 102, *103*, *106*

Calendar 5, *21*, 21, 24
  Book of Common Prayer 24
  commentary 13
candle in baptism service 69, *69*, *72*
candle in initiation service 69, *78–9*
candle, Easter 69
Candlemas, *see* Presentation of Christ
Canon B14 *14*
Canon B23 *73*, *80*
Canon B24 *80*
Canon B37 *88*
Canon B5 *15*, *18*, *44*
Canon C26 *110*
Canons B43 and B44, *18*

142

Index

sermon *31, 34, 49*, 50, *56, see also* preaching
 in a baptism service *67, 71–2*
 in a funeral *102*, 104
 in a marriage service 91, *92–3*
 in a Thanksgiving for a Child 96
Service of the Word, *see* A Service of the Word
Signing with the cross 68, *70, 71–2, 77–8*
silence 5, *40*, 40, 48, *100*, 118
Sing God's Glory 125
Social Justice and Responsibility 9, 29
songs, *see* hymns
Special Occasions 9, 29, *32*, 42
sponsors 68, *80*
standard volume, see main volume
Stations of the Cross, *see* Way of the Cross
Stations of the Resurrection 11, *24*
suicide *101*
Sunday by Sunday 125
Sunday by Sunday: Music for the Second Service Lectionary 126
Sunday volume, see main volume
supplementary consecration *61*
supplementary texts 5, 10, 19, *53*, 54, 57, 66, *87*, 88, *99*
supporting friends in Thanksgiving for a Child 96–7

Team Ministry 84
testimony *71, 77*
Thanksgiving for Holy Baptism 66
Thanksgiving for Marriage 90
Thanksgiving for the Gift of a Child 5, 6, 12, 65, 66, *72*, 73, 82, *83*, 83, 95–8
Thanksgiving for the Healing Ministry of the Church 86
Thanksgiving Prayer for a Child *70, 72*
The Christian Year: Calendar, Lectionary and Collects 9, 13, 29

themes 9, 29, *34*, 44, 58, 124
 in *New Patterns for Worship* 21, *34*
Time to Pray 109
Times and Seasons, see Common Worship: Times and Seasons
traditional language 1, 57
 collects 5, 9, 10, 29, 41, 42, 43, *43*
 Holy Communion 51–2, *58*, 84
 Lord's Prayer *114, 122*
 marriage vows *90, 93*
 Night Prayer *110*, 125
transferences of holy days 28
tribute, at a funeral *102*
Trinitarian ascription *53*, 55
trinitarian ending to collects *40, 41*
Trinity Sunday 25

Unity of the Church 9, 29, 114

vigil 66, 105
Vigil Office 115
Visual Liturgy 14, 123–5, 126
vows
 in marriage service *89, 90,* 91, *93, 94*
 renewal of baptismal *74*
 renewal of marriage 90

water 68, *71, 75, 78*
Way of the Cross 11, *24*
website
 Church House Publishing 37
 Church of England *3*, 13, 14, *19*, 37, 38, 43, 62, *112*
 Transforming Worship *61*
 Visual Liturgy Live 124
wedding anniversary 90
weddings, *see* marriage
Welcome, in marriage service 91, *92*
Welcome, in initiation services *72, 79*
Wholeness and Healing 6, 7, 10, 66, 82, 83, 84–8

youth *31, 47*